FROM THESE MEN

TRANSLATED BY

PHILIP SIMPSON

Seven Founders of the State of Israel

SHIMON PERES

WYNDHAM BOOKS
New York

Published by *Wyndham Books*
A Simon & Schuster Division of
Gulf & Western Corporation
Simon & Schuster Building
1230 Avenue of the Americas
New York, New York 10020
WYNDHAM and colophon are
trademarks of Simon & Schuster
Designed by Dianne Pinkowitz
Manufactured in the United States of America
Printed and bound by Fairfield Graphics, Inc.
10 9 8 7 6 5 4 3 2 1
Library of Congress Cataloging in Publication Data
Peres, Shimon, date.
    From these men.
    Translation of Lekh 'im ha-anashim.
    CONTENTS: David Ben-Gurion.—Levi Eshkol.—Berl
Katznelson. [etc.]
    1. Israel—Biography. I. Title.
DS126.6.A2P4713   956.94'05'0922 [B]   79-2560
ISBN 0-671-61016-3

CONTENTS

PREFACE

MANY ARE THE PEOPLE—leaders, teachers and friends —whom I have known in my lifetime. A few of them I wish to describe here. They live on in my memory as centers of light and warmth, as men who helped to create the climate of our times.

I have chosen to commit to paper my recollections of them, not in lines of latitude and longitude, but rather in the form, according to contours of length and breadth and height, of a sketchbook, presenting the profiles that have lingered in my memory even after the men have passed away.

Every one of us bears in his heart the image of people who are head and shoulders above the rest, or people who are at the root of things, or people who have given charm and excitement to our lives. Just as it is impossible to love a homeland in the abstract, without being acquainted with its soil and its scenery, so it is impossible to love a people in the abstract—you must know its history and the men and women who shaped its unique form.

The seven men whom I have chosen for my book are like the seven branches of a candelabrum. And I have chosen them not only because of their singularity, but also on account of the link, explicit and implicit, that connects them; fundamentally they are made of one piece, a part of the fabric of our lives.

With David Ben-Gurion I worked for seventeen years without a pause, sometimes days and nights without a break. I knew him well, and I am bound to say that not only did I see him as the greatest Jew of our generation, but my admiration for him continued to grow throughout the years of our acquaintance. I did not hesitate to admit this in his lifetime and today, in retrospect, I am proud that I recognized his greatness and called it by its name.

With Levi Eshkol I both worked and lived in close proximity of place (he was a member of Degania "B" and I of Alumot; and later, when I was his deputy at the Ministry of Defense, we sat in adjacent offices) and proximity of viewpoint (he was reckoned an eminent activist). I always loved the way in which his wonderful sense of humor was combined with a tireless creative instinct. There were good days, when relations between Ben-Gurion and Eshkol, both professional and personal, were amicable and close, and these were followed by days of crisis. I played a role of sorts, not always consciously and not always willingly, both during the days of friendship and then during the time of estrangement.

I was a young man when I first met Berl Katznelson and his influence on the formation of my opinions and beliefs—and those of my entire generation—was decisive. He inspired and encouraged in us a deep attachment to literature, to poetry, to all spiritual things. He was our teacher.

With Nathan Alterman I had a dual relationship: as an admirer of his poetry and as a close personal friend. I first became acquainted with his poetry; later, when I met the poet, I was equally impressed by his personality—a personality both profound and humble. Every encounter was like a celebration to me. I always looked forward to seeing him. And I was never disappointed.

Ernst David Bergmann was in my view the most distinguished representative of scientific talent that our people has ever produced. We worked together in the Ministry of Defense, where Bergmann served as Chief Scientific Adviser and Chairman of the Atomic Energy Commission in the Prime Minister's Office, and we forged a strong and lasting friendship. Sometimes he lost his temper with me when he thought that we were not exploiting our scientific potential to the full, and sometimes I lost my temper with him, when I felt that he was going too far and in too many directions. Nevertheless, I believe that our collaboration produced impressive results of great value to both the people and the country. Our disagreements in the professional sphere never injured our personal friendship nor diminished my admiration for him.

Moshe Haviv was my friend and companion in an experiment unique in the public life of Israel, the formation of the Rafi party. He fell in the Six Day War on the Golan Heights, and with his death a great hope was extinguished. Like so many others of his generation, he never had the opportunity to realize his full potential. I have always felt that it is people like Moshe, remarkable people living, sometimes in obscurity at the grass-roots level of the nation, who constitute the real wealth of the nation, a part of its human fabric, the rock on which it is founded. It is of such men that Alterman once said: "These are the people who make things grow."

Yonatan Netanyahu was the hero of a thrilling episode, one of the most impressive feats in the annals of Israel. By setting the seal of his heroism— and his sacrifice—on the Entebbe Raid he made it "Operation Yonatan." I decided to conclude the book with his portrait because he is a fine representative of a younger generation, and also because I remember that on the eve of the operation, in the darkness of the camp where his unit was preparing to go into action, we discussed the poetry of Nathan Alterman. I felt that a mysterious circle had somehow been completed.

Preface

It may be that I shall be criticized for the lack of shade in the pictures that I have drawn, on the grounds that an authentic picture depends on the contrast of light and shadow. However, I believe that shadows are not what are required for a portrait; we tend to exaggerate them as it is. In the final and true analysis, it is the credit side that we are judged by, and it is this that gives meaning to our lives and justifies our willingness to struggle for Life, whatever the circumstances and whatever the outcome.

I am not unaware of the theory which claims that the heart of man is essentially evil. But I am convinced that Israel is the story of man at his best. This belief is the torch that guides our footsteps and illuminates our paths, we who walk like men and with men.

Tel Aviv,   SHIMON PERES
March 1979

I am mature enough to understand that people are no less important than ideas.

MARY MCCARTHY

DAVID BEN-GURION
In Strength and Spirit

The fate of Israel depends on her strength and her justice.

DAVID BEN-GURION

I REMEMBER ONE DAY accompanying David Ben-Gurion on a visit to Dimona. Dimona was a place very close to his heart, for a number of reasons: its location in the northern part of the Negev; the new form of settlement which the town represented; the settlers, who were immigrants from North Africa; its proximity to the Atomic Research Establishment; the grove named after his wife Paula. "The Old Man" was in high spirits.

We visited the primary school and Ben-Gurion invited the pupils, eleven- and twelve-year olds, to ask him questions. A statuesque young girl, her dark eyes flashing with excitement, put up her hand and Ben-Gurion nodded to her. She asked: "Mr. Ben-Gurion, at what time in your life did you feel the greatest satisfaction?" Ben-Gurion smiled to himself, and suddenly his face took on a serious expression and he said: "What is satisfaction? What is the good of it? If a man becomes satisfied, what is he to do then? A man who is satisfied no longer yearns, no longer dreams, no longer creates, no longer makes demands. No, I have never known a single moment of satisfaction."

David Ben-Gurion went to his grave with perhaps a fuller record of achievements than any other man of this century. Great achievements, but no satisfaction. From his childhood to the end of his life he displayed a formidable willpower, that neither Nature nor Man could deflect. Ben-Gurion was never content with the achievement of the present. Even after all the changes that affected our people and all the victories they won, he continued to insist that the establishment of the State of Israel was as yet incomplete; it was not enough simply to gather in the Jews of the Diaspora—we must rise still higher in order to become a nation of quality, a nation of distinction. He feared that the security of Israel was not something that could be taken for granted; in spite of all the strength that she had amassed, Israel must work tirelessly to guarantee her peace, both present and future. He felt that military victories were not enough—peace must be made with our Arab neighbors, so that we might become a nation contributing to the progress and development of the whole of the Middle East.

His vision was the vision of a man of spirit, and yet there was no man who understood reality as well as he. Reality as it is, and as it should be—a chariot covering vast new distances when harnessed to the horses of vision. His horizons were sown with demands and his achievements—only stations on the way.

Dimona was such a station, a tender fledgling which when the time came would spread its wings and fly in this landscape that had once been nothing but desert.

In Ben-Gurion the two most important ingredients of true leadership were combined: earthy realism and sky-scraping vision. He never deceived himself or others with regard to the difficulties to be expected on the way, but as long as he lived he was never for one moment deflected from the fundamental ideas that guided his actions. His whole life was dedicated to the idea of the salvation of the Jewish people in their own land. This single idea gave to his life all its richness and variety. In contrast with other great leaders of this century, he did not try to direct an existing reality along a new path, but strove to create a new reality from within an abstract vision.

All the great leaders of our century: Lenin, Churchill, De Gaulle, Mao Tse-tung, were born in their own countries, they all grappled with a certain reality existing in their homelands, or with dangers threatening them from outside. Ben-Gurion was the only one among them who was not born in his own land; he was the bearer of a dream before he was the representative of a people. He was born before he even had a homeland; he was a war leader before he had an army, and he was a statesman before he had a state. In the space of two generations he had traveled and had led his people over a course that other leaders and other peoples have taken whole centuries to traverse.

Along the whole of this road he led the way, he marched at the head and only rarely stood to the side. The spirit of pioneering appealed to him more than the conventions. Throughout his life his step was brisk and urgent, on a road that he himself paved, never deterred by chasms or summits, not allowing himself to be deceived by mirages and not retreating at the advice of friends or opponents.

From his earliest childhood and throughout his life he was (in Ahad Ha-Am's words) in a state of constant warfare "with the way of the world." He could afford to do battle with the way of the world, because temperamentally he was well equipped for such a fight. He was inspired by a vibrant love of the truth, he had a will of iron, he was endowed with a rare talent for judgment, and his wisdom and morality were never at variance with each other.

His friend since childhood, Shlomo Lavie, described him succinctly and eloquently as "A man in whom an impulsive wisdom is blended with a deep sense of morality, and who sometimes is inspired with the Spirit of God." Or as Ben-Gurion described himself in a more earthy fashion (in a letter that he sent to his father after arriving on the shores of Eretz Israel): "I am healthy, vigorous and full of faith."

Even in his childhood it was recognized that here was a man destined for great things. At a very early age he knew his own mind. "I became a Zionist at the age of four," Ben-Gurion once told me, and I believed him. He decided to speak Hebrew. He changed his name. He established an organization called "Ezra" and while still a boy he set out alone for the land of destiny. No childish games, no country walks, no social recreations—the young man bypassed all the normal activities of his age group in his single-minded pursuit of the mission to which he was destined.

Ben-Gurion was a man of singular appearance; although small in stature, for some reason he gave the impression of being very tall; his head was large, with fierce and penetrating eyes and a vigorous, stubborn chin. There was something leonine about him, both formidable and attractive. It was as if his legs were made for running, not walking, and his hands were especially large, the expressive and creative hands of an artist. There was nothing soft in his appearance, which radiated a strange and captivating personal charm. It was as if his figure was carved from a single ingot; the only form of decoration that he had was his mane of hair, and with this the whole was crystallized and sharply focused, without the need for any extraneous ornament.

There were never two Ben-Gurions: the young Ben-Gurion and the old, or the private Ben-Gurion and the public, or Ben-Gurion the leader and Ben-Gurion the man of the people. When he was young he was already mature and in old age he retained the vivaciousness of a young man. When he opened his eyes in the morning he saw his people before him, for in his family he saw a part of his people (even his impassioned love letters to Paula represent an unflagging effort at enticing a Jewish girl to savor the enchantments of Israel). And in the basement of Brenner House he used to argue with the unemployed with that same seriousness he displayed in debates with his colleagues in the Cabinet. He hated falseness and did not know how to pretend.

Although there was no ambivalence in his personality, Ben-Gurion stored within himself a coalition of forces and tendencies, which used to appear unexpectedly, in varying degrees of intensity, making him an enigma in the eyes of friends and opponents alike. It was said of him that he was a master tactician, and yet sometimes he was capable of childlike innocence. It was said of him that he was remote from day-to-day experiences, and he caused astonishment with his detailed knowledge of people and situations. He was reckoned to be a stern realist but at times he showed extreme sentimentality.

All his life he remembered better than any of us and he knew much more than we knew. He drew his information from the most varied sources, such as rare books, the works of forgotten journalists, extraordinary people, situations buried in obscure and distant landscapes—all these things appealed to his exceptional intuition.

When he read the Bible, he was capable of seeing its heroes standing in front of him. And when he looked around him, it was as if he was reading a chapter from the Bible.

A case in point was the occasion when Chief of Staff Yigael Yadin, who was a close friend of Ben-Gurion's, resigned from his post following a violent disagreement between them over the size of the regular army, with Ben-Gurion insisting that manning levels be kept down to a minimum for reasons of economy. This dispute led to Yadin's resignation, which Ben-Gurion accepted with great reluctance. Yadin's deputy, Mordechai Makleff, was appointed in his place. Yadin was a charismatic leader; Makleff was his loyal deputy. Now their positions were reversed, with Yadin becoming an officer in the reserves, under the orders of his former subordinate. The situation caused some embarrassment, and at the ceremony in which the deputy took over his duties, the atmosphere was rather tense. Ben-Gurion winked mischievously at the two men and opening the book of the *Aggadah* (rabbinical homilies) he read aloud to us the chapter relating to the death of Moses:

> The Holy One said to Moses: every generation has its preachers, every generation its administrators and every generation

its leaders. Until now it has been your lot to serve me, and now it is the turn of your pupil Joshua to serve me. . . . Moses rose and hastened to the door of Joshua's tent. Joshua sat there preaching, and Moses stooped and laid his hand on his heart, and Joshua's eyes were dimmed and he did not see him. . . . Then Moses cried out saying: a hundred deaths and not one sign of jealousy!

This parallel situation, of Moses and Joshua as flesh and blood on the one hand, and of the Chief of Staff and his deputy as figures from the *Aggadah* on the other, made the past and the present into a single fabric, legend and reality inseparable, the quality of the words unimpaired by the order of events, the gulf of time.

When we held our tongues—he made his views public; when we talked at length—he maintained his silence. This man, who radiated from within himself millions of words and thoughts appropriate to every aspect of life and action, was on the one hand a man of strong self-discipline, on the other an incorrigible romantic in regard to everything new. He knew how to master his own instincts and also how to conquer new territory that no man had trod before him. The words of Jeremiah, "to walk in ways that are not paved," had a special appeal for him. He did not hesitate to express unconventional views, but he hardly ever made the mistake of putting forward unconsidered opinions.

Although he saw the desert as the most beautiful of landscapes, he believed that it was possible to change the climate by means of afforestation and he was prepared to cover the entire land surface with poplar trees. He was convinced that sea water could provide the necessary irrigation for a flourishing agricultural economy.

He believed that China would become a world power. He foresaw a united Europe. He believed that in the place of nation-states, communities of nations would arise.

At the same time, he was careful to express opinions about individuals only when engaged in polemic or debate. He had no time for trivialities or gossip. He rejected passing enthusiasms. I was with him when the news arrived that the United Nations had voted in favor of the establishment of the State of Israel. All over the country there was jubilation and dancing in the streets. Ben-Gurion stayed in his room, as if he had no interest in what was going on. We suspected that he was ignoring the event because he had a low opinion of the United Nations Organization. But his explanation was different: "Now they are dancing, but tomorrow we shall find ourselves at war."

Apparently there was a contradiction between Ben-Gurion's formidable public image and the true character of the man as revealed to those of us who worked with him. His external manner could be stormy; his inner temperament was calm and moderate.

Every working day with Ben-Gurion was like a festival to us. We did not come to his office in Sabbath clothes, but we were always in a Sabbath mood. We never knew what the day would produce, but we could be sure that it would not be sterile. There was bound to be some action or drama; no day with Ben-Gurion was dull.

And when we came into his presence we would be amazed, for the thousandth time, to find ourselves confronted by a man of equable temperament and high spirits, with an ear attentive to almost everything. "When I'm agitated," Ben-Gurion told me once, "it's a sign that I'm calm, and when I'm calm, it's a sign that I'm agitated." I can remember seeing Ben-Gurion cheerful or furious, agreeable or argumentative, but I never saw him moody or bored. He was not influenced by the prevailing atmosphere —he created it.

I remember how one morning, at the beginning of the War of Independence, the General Staff Headquarters in Ramat Gan came under bombardment. Shells dropped in the courtyard of the little house where Ben-Gurion was sitting and one of the sentries at the door was critically injured. I hurried to his office with Nehemiah Argov, who was then Ben-Gurion's aide de camp, and we begged him to go down to the bomb shelter. He contented himself with putting on a steel helmet, then looking at us with an expression of childish astonishment, he said: "Look, I'm in the middle of writing something, how can I break off now?" But when he was told that the sentry had been wounded he left his papers and came running out to help us with the stretcher. He insisted on being one of the bearers and would not leave the injured man until he was safely in the hospital. He saw no reason why bombs should determine his way of life—he determined it! And the fact that they were falling on the roof of his house was quite irrelevant in comparison with the urgency of his work.

Apart from his even temper—and agitation was a part of his evenness—I suppose that the thing which always impressed us most was his diligence. He wrote his letters and speeches himself. He even filed them. He did everything himself, from filling his fountain pen from the inkwell in the drawer of his desk to cutting out the newspaper clippings that he needed with his own pair of scissors. On his desk lay a Bible and a concordance. Between the pages of the Bible were slips of paper marking passages to be used in articles or speeches. He used the concordance for locating suitable quotations. He searched for books himself and he always knew when and where a book that he wanted was due to be published. He loved browsing through his extensive library, which contained some thirty thousand books.

Books were more important to him than food, and his passion for acquiring books sometimes led to bizarre situations. When we were on our way to Paris for an official visit, he asked me if I knew the city well. "More or less," I replied. Then he asked: "Do you know where the Boulevard Raspé is?" "Yes,

I know it." "Well, then," he said, "when we arrive in Paris, that's where we are going."

I asked him what business he had in mind, suggesting that perhaps I could see to it on his behalf and save him the trouble. But no, it was something very urgent and he had to deal with it himself. It was only after a lot of probing from me that the puzzle was solved. About a year before he had obtained the first volume of a French edition of *History of Western Philosophy*. He had recently received a catalogue from the publisher in which it was announced that the second volume was due to be published and would be available immediately after publication at a major bookshop in the Boulevard Raspé.

An even more instructive incident was one involving Golda Meir. The infant State was at war and suffering from an embargo on the supply of arms. Even if sources of arms had been available, we did not have the money with which to buy them. Ben-Gurion believed that acquiring resources for the purchase of arms was a project of first priority, and he decided to make a fund-raising visit to the United States. This caused his colleagues a great deal of concern. The absence of Ben-Gurion, the nation's leader, at the very height of the war, even for a few days, seemed to them a tragic mistake. Golda Meir attacked his decision vociferously and demanded that she make the journey instead, insisting that nobody was capable of taking his place at home, but that she could deputize for him in the United States.

There was a stormy debate in the National Council, and when a vote was taken Ben-Gurion was overruled and Golda's appointment to the mission was approved. Ben-Gurion was incensed at this decision. Golda flew from the besieged city of Jerusalem to Tel Aviv by Piper Cub, in readiness for her flight to the United States.

She checked into a small hotel on the seashore. That evening the hotel manager knocked on the door of her room and announced that an unexpected visitor was waiting for her downstairs: David Ben-Gurion. Golda was much moved at the thought that, in spite of their quarrel, he had taken the trouble to come and say good-bye to her.

Ben-Gurion shook her hand warmly and wished her success in her vital mission. Then, somewhat embarrassed, he produced a slip of paper on which he had written a list of books that he wanted her to try to obtain for him in the United States.

Ben-Gurion kept a diary, written out by hand in exercise books with blank covers. He recorded meticulously every item of information that he heard, every instruction that he gave. His able and dedicated assistant, Chaim Israeli, was adept at following these notes and classifying them into items of history and items of present-day concern. Ben-Gurion was always busy and he always had the time to deal with things that he considered urgent. We once estimated that he had written replies to thirty letters in less than one hour.

His attitude toward time was one of total respect. He hated carelessness and he detested waste. He arrived everywhere punctually and he would complain at any delay. He was not in favor of lengthy meals or of pleasantries for their own sake, and wherever possible he took pains to avoid entertainments, concerts, plays and exhibitions. He insisted that he had no time for such frivolities and his opinion of modern poetry was most irreverent. For example, he used to claim that it was possible to read an *avant-garde* poem not according to the order of the lines but from the bottom upward, without noticing any change in the sense. His taste in art was for the monumental; the sculptures and paintings of Michelangelo appealed to him especially.

It was not only delay that he detested; he was equally averse to postponement. In postponement he saw evasion of decision or work-shyness; everything that can be done today must be done immediately. He used to present us with questions formulated in writing and expect answers to them that very day. In correct timing he saw a combination of work-efficiency and political wisdom, and for him correct timing usually meant immediate action. When he decided, in spite of great and growing pressure from the United States, to transfer the seat of government from Tel Aviv to Jerusalem, his colleagues tried hard to persuade him to postpone the transfer, if only for a week, but all their efforts were in vain. He would have none of it; it must be done at once, this very minute. And he described his "Biltmore Program" as a scheme for the establishment of a Jewish State *at once,* in other words, a vision with a date attached to it. He insisted that time could work either for us or against us, it all depended on how it was used.

His attitude toward punctuality sprang from another great love of his life, a central love—the love of truth. Ben-Gurion was prepared to condone a great many things, but he was never prepared to compromise nor to abandon the truth. From himself and from others he demanded knowledge of the truth, telling of the truth, pursuit of the truth and belief in the truth. When one of his aides failed in this respect, he immediately lost all credibility in Ben-Gurion's eyes. The truth consists above all in clarity. When he was informed of something and told that "he said such and such" he would interrupt immediately and ask: "Who are you talking about? When and where did he say that and what *exactly* did he say?" In his writings there are very few examples of the use of "etc." or "and so forth." All things require precision.

Truth is ageless. Truth that is backed by the authority of time—that too needs to be closely scrutinized. He even read the Bible with critical eyes: was it really David who defeated Goliath? Or did David perhaps claim for himself the heroic deed of another general, Elhanan Ben-Yaari, of whom the Bible testifies that "he smote Goliath of Gath" (Samuel II, xxi, 19)?

One day in 1961 Ben-Gurion summoned a meeting of journalists in Sokolov House in Tel Aviv.

This must have been the most extraordinary speech ever made by a Prime Minister to an audience of journalists anywhere. The central issue under discussion was most topical—the Exodus from Egypt. He began his address with the following words:

> The establishment of the State of Israel and the War of Independence have shed a new light on my understanding of the Bible, and after examining it afresh in the light of the reality of the War of Independence and the resettlement of Israel in our time, I have been moved to pose questions to which Biblical commentators throughout the ages have paid insufficient attention.

He then went on to put forward "thirty intriguing questions," beginning with "Why did Terah and his family leave Ur of the Chaldees, a developed and fertile country, to go to thc land of Canaan?" and ending with "How could the grandchildren of the seventy couples who went down into Egypt have taken possession of the lands of the Amorite king Sihon and Og king of Bashan to the East of the Jordan and defeated the majority of the peoples of Canaan in battle? Such a thing would have been impossible. They were obliged not only to conquer territory but also to settle in it. How could they settle? How many were they at that time?"

And Ben-Gurion was not satisfied until he had proved that the "six hundred thousand men, excluding children'' who left Egypt and went to the land of Canaan ''were not six hundred thousand but six hundred families, since the word meaning 'thousand' is also used in the Bible for the concept of 'family.' As Rabbi Kimhi says: '*Alfey* (thousands) is related to *aluf*, which means lord and master.' From which it follows that heads of thousands of Israelites are heads of families of Israelites.''

Truth does not reveal itself in the marketplace. It does not present itself voluntarily—it must be sought after, pursued in the depths of history, in the infinite spaces of the universe, in the complexities of mankind. When it is encountered, it is not to be avoided, and Ben-Gurion was quite ruthless in his perception of the truth of things, and most eager to discover it again and again. The pursuit of truth made Ben-Gurion a great student, perhaps the greatest student produced by our people among the leaders of the new era. His books testify to this—the thousands that he read and the dozens that he wrote. As a student he was both assisted and plagued by two conflicting qualities: on the one hand, he was imbued with the curiosity of a distinguished intellectual; on the other, he was imbued with the spirit of a man of action.

Intellectuals tend to live in a world where doubt is a frequent and regular visitor, whereas men of action are obliged to overcome doubt, make positive statements and take firm decisions. Ben-Gurion, who never satisfied his thirst for knowledge, was always curious, always insatiable, but he never allowed doubt to interfere with the need for decision. He was capable of learning anything without later forming a distinct opinion of it. Sometimes his opinions preceded his knowledge, and then he sought corroboration in his studies; sometimes his knowledge preceded his opinions, and then he would attempt to formulate new conclusions. And in any case, neither knowledge nor opinion was left in isolation; his reading and his writing are evidence of this. He read, examined and interpreted. Then he decided and acted. Finally he recorded in writing what he had learned and what he had done.

When Ben-Gurion decided to immigrate to Eretz Israel, he immersed himself in geographical books and read thousands of pages in his quest for information. Later he toured the country on foot. Finally, in 1917, he collaborated with his friend Yitzhak Ben-Zvi in publishing a book on the geography of Eretz Israel, *Eretz-Israel in Vergangenheit und Gegenwart.*

In his researches he also encountered the problem of the Arab inhabitants of the country, and in 1931 he published his book *We and Our Neighbours,* which was remarkable not only for its array of facts and findings, but also for its accurate predictions of future events. In this case his opinions preceded his knowledge. In old age he studied just as keenly as he had in his youth. Toward the end of his life he developed a passionate interest in biology, physics and chemistry, and these sciences exercised a profound influence on his thought and behavior.

The public life of Ben-Gurion was divided into three basic phases: approximately fifteen years as leader of the Histadrut (Trade Unions Federation); fifteen years as head of the Jewish Agency; and fifteen years as Prime Minister. His reading and writing accompanied him in all these functions and they formed the background and perspective to every period of his life.

In his Histadrut period he read a great deal of Socialist and revolutionary literature, as well as books about mass psychology. He once told me that he used to spend whole days in the New York Public Library reading psychology books, and he said that he had read dozens of volumes of Lenin's writings. It was at this time that he published his book of collected essays, *From Class to Peoplehood*, whose title gives an indication of its contents.

In his Jewish Agency period he was much concerned with the historiosophy of the Jewish people and the prerequisites of a Jewish State. At that time he returned to his reading of Jewish history and he developed a special affinity with the works of Shimon Dubnow and Ezekiel Kaufmann. Years later he published his own version of the history of our people, *The Jews in Their Land*. I believe that it was during this same period that he was introduced to Greek philosophy, where he discovered the intellectual basis for a just State, a State founded on philosophical principles.

In the third period, as Prime Minister and Minister of Defense, concern for the security of the State took precedence over all else. Ben-Gurion took great pains to prepare himself for the role of Minister of Defense; there was hardly a single defense or army expert whose opinions Ben-Gurion did not examine meticulously, and there was hardly a single book on military history or strategic technique that escaped his attention. A special favorite of his was Thucydides' account of the Peloponnesian War. In his view Thucydides was an expert at describing all the strategic issues involved: topology, popular morale, the quality of the enemy and tactical planning. He read the memoirs of veterans of Hashomer and the Haganah, the Jewish Brigade and the dissident movements, and it is unlikely that he overlooked the memoirs of a single general or statesman.

In his war speeches there are echoes of his specialized researches in all of these fields.

Naturally, the Bible served as a powerful and inspiring backdrop to all of his reading. There he found the best of all sources of Socialist belief, of the Zionist message, of the art of war and of the yearning for peace. He loved the book of Amos especially, with its protest against those who seek "to buy the poor with silver and the beggar with a pair of shoes"; its belief that "on that day I shall raise the fallen tent of David"; its fear lest "the trumpet be blown in the street and the people tremble not"; and its vision of the meeting between "the ploughman and the reaper, the treader of grapes and the sower of seed, while the mountains drip sweet juices and the hills melt from fruitfulness."

After the establishment of the State he turned

his attention toward science, in which he saw a basis for the supremacy of quality. In his scientific reading he quickly became engrossed in biology and the nature of the human brain was a matter of boundless curiosity to him. He saw this as the greatest riddle of the universe and the greatest of the creations of Providence. I fear that this late study of biology, begun at a time when he was already approaching old age, may have hastened his decision to retire from the Government. It appears that the brain, losing approximately a hundred million cells every day, is the first bodily organ to decay. Ben-Gurion was deeply afraid that his brain might be deteriorating; he suffered real physical agony whenever he forgot a date, the name of a place or a person.

He saw this as an alarm signal. Ben-Gurion was a student of books and his own teacher. He was drawn toward Buddhism, conceiving it to be a system whereby the spirit controls the body, whereby the mind can overcome the caprices of flesh and blood. He sometimes used to quote Ben-Sira, and one of the latter's proverbs was a permanent fixture on his desk: "Do not seek to be a ruler if you have not the strength to subdue caprice." His studies were in a sense "the strength that subdues caprice." Through literary sources he acquired a group of teachers at whose feet he loved to kneel; they deepened his sense of humility and fortified his powers of judgment; they came to his assistance and from them he demanded historical assessments and philosophical contentions.

He liked to learn from the source. He was suspicious of translations and commentaries. He knew a number of languages, some of which he learned in childhood (Yiddish, Russian, Hebrew), some of which he acquired through study and travel (Turkish, Arabic, English, German). He also learned French and Spanish to gain an understanding of other cultures, and he learned classical Greek to gain an understanding of the ancient world; he wanted to study the works of Socrates and Plato in the original and he also wanted to make the acquaintance of Don Quixote from firsthand experience. He learned Spanish from his secretary, Yitzhak Navon.* As he read—so he studied. He studied, but was not overwhelmed. He absorbed, and was never satisfied. His obstinate spirit sometimes rebelled against the high status accorded to great writers and he sought to translate the logic of the ancients into the terms of the present, to put it at the disposal of his passionate faith.

The picture of Ben-Gurion as a scholar will never be complete unless we recall the fact that he was blessed with a phenomenal memory. Ben-Gurion told us that he was capable of returning from a four-hour meeting with the High Commissioner and later repeating every word said on both sides. Sometimes we had the impression that he remembered every single thing that had happened to him every day of his life, and that he was able to quote by heart the proceedings of long-past conferences and forgot-

* Yitzhak Navon is now President of Israel.

ten institutions. But the occasion on which his remarkable memory astonished me most was one of quite secondary importance.

In the early sixties, a high-ranking visitor from Nigeria arrived in the country. Ben-Gurion invited him to a banquet and as was customary made a speech in honor of his guest. In his speech he referred to the development of Nigeria and described in glowing terms that country's rapid strides toward progress. In support of his argument he quoted statistics illustrating the growth over the past twenty years in the number of schools, the volume of railway traffic and the population of the capital, Lagos. I was amused at what Ben-Gurion had to say and furthermore I was curious to know how he had prepared this speech and whence he had acquired these figures. Admittedly, Nigeria now has a Year Book, but how did he know the figures relating to the forties? After the banquet I approached him and asked how he had obtained this plethora of statistics. His reply astounded me: it emerged that on one occasion during the Second World War he had flown from the United States to Eretz Israel in an American Air Force plane. To avoid the danger of encountering German aircraft the American plane was diverted via Africa and there it made an overnight stop. "There was nothing for me to do at the airbase," said Ben-Gurion, "so I picked up a copy of the Nigeria Year Book. I read it from cover to cover, and that is how I remember the figures." To remember statistical data picked up during a wayside halt and to repeat them years later—is this not an extraordinary phenomenon?

His memory was remarkable—and it was not confined to his own experience but to the actions and attitudes of others as well. His wonderful memory and his aggressive instinct made him an unusually formidable polemicist. He saw himself as the successor of Amos, in the sense of the command: "Prophet, go flee to the land of Judah, and there eat bread and there prophesy!" But in this respect Ben-Gurion was different from the majority of the leaders of our times, with their eagerness to ingratiate themselves with the public, to mollify, appease, compromise. Public relations, public image, public acceptability—all these were foreign to his nature, while his relations with the press were at the same time cordial and tendentious. He read the newspapers and he argued with them. But he never gave in to them. His real public relations were conducted not with a view to the pages of newspapers, but with a view to the pages of history.

Opposition, rivalry, controversy—all these were spurs to his fighting spirit; he used to marshal all his intellectual forces, reconnoiter the enemies' defenses, identify their weak points and charge at them with dazzling and remorseless ferocity.

Ben-Gurion had so many qualities of his own that he had no need to be jealous of other people, but he was jealous of his opinions and every one of his campaigns was undertaken in the spirit of a crusade. He was not impressed by the greatness or the importance of his opponents. The greater his opponent, the more ferocious his attack.

Such was his attack on the British Empire. In *Contesting the Ruler,* one of the finest speeches he ever made, he called upon us to fight the Nazis as if we had no quarrel with the British, and to fight the British as if we had no quarrel with the Nazis.

The dead Marx and the living Stalin were his constant and inveterate targets. Both Marxism and Stalinism, for which there were overt and covert sympathizers within the Labor movement, he assessed with devastating perception. I remember the sensation that he caused when he described Stalin as "a Georgian hooligan" and referred to Marx as "an anti-Marxist."

He engaged in controversy with almost all of his Zionist and Socialist colleagues: with Weizmann and Jabotinsky, with Katznelson and Sprinzak, with Tabenkin and Yaari, with Begin and Sneh, with Harzfeld and Eshkol. Many people suspected Ben-Gurion of acting out of vindictiveness in these campaigns, but I am sure that he was convinced that it was solely a case of argument for its own sake, argument to be conducted ruthlessly, as a means of shedding clear and immediate light on the path to be followed. His fervor arose from the ideological extreme, not the personal. He needed controversy as a means of arriving at the truth, the truth of today and tomorrow, a truth which had as yet neither supporters nor sympathizers, a vision without a base. That is why he sometimes adopted the tactics of the duel, identifying the leader of the opposing camp and aiming at him the full force of his verbal stone slinging.

It seems to me that his very opponents were the ones who felt the greatest sense of loss at Ben-Gurion's departure from the public stage. There was no longer anyone with whom to argue fiercely and boldly; his fighting spirit was no longer a factor in debate and the political drama gave way to a sterile silence, or turned into a babbling marketplace. We might say of him, in Plutarch's words:

> The events which followed intensified and clarified the feeling of sorrow at the death of Pericles. Even those to whom his great strength had been a burden, those whom he had overshadowed, admitted when he had departed from the scene and they were faced with other orators and demagogues, that never again would they see a character of such precious moderation and such eminent humility; and that power which in their envy they had described as autocracy and tyranny, seemed to them now the very cornerstone of the survival of the State.

When the late Mr. Eshkol became Prime Minister, Ben-Gurion's advice to him was: "Eshkol, do not be a compromiser." Ben-Gurion made many compromises, but he never compromised himself. Compromise for the sake of decision in the field of action, yes; weak-minded departure from principle, no.

If we look at the gallery of Ben-Gurion's friends, we shall see that he never deserted a single comrade, just as he never deserted an opponent. In the Knesset his slogan was: "No deals with Herut or the Communists." This was a hurtful statement, and quite unjust too, since he was clearly at fault in linking the two together. And in the Labor movement, which he was eager to unite, he laid down principles that made unity impossible. He disagreed with Tabenkin on the issue of securing the integrity of the land at the price of losing sovereignty over a part of it; he disagreed with Yaari on the issue of a binational state, which he saw as an unrealistic objective. He quarreled with both of them over Marxism and "the orientation to the world of tomorrow." He could not come to terms with the existence of factions within his own party, and he was particularly perturbed by the rise of the Gush, a bloc which in effect controlled Mapai. To the sorrow of many he canceled the Workers' Education Scheme, closed down the Employment Office of the Histadrut, and demanded changes in the electoral system. I ask myself the question: how did he manage to summon up the strength to wage such tireless and unremitting internal and external warfare, against both colleagues and opponents—and at the same time maintain a quite exceptional *joie de vivre,* a glowing and all-embracing optimism?

His friends and colleagues knew for a fact that

if Ben-Gurion gave his word, he would act upon it. He would be deterred by no obstacles, threats or dangers, whatever the outcome. Thus his views were not only clear, they were also steadfast.

Ben-Gurion abhorred the Diaspora. The Diaspora, exile, the ghetto, all these were to him a distressing aberration in the life of the Jewish people. After the First and Second Temples a Third Temple must arise, and what happened in the wake of the Destruction was in itself a part of the Destruction. Only thanks to their indomitable spirit had the Jewish people succeeded in maintaining their existence over a period of two thousand years. They had survived, but their survival had not been creative. He refused to take consolation in the fact that his tiny people had produced great men like Spinoza, Marx and Einstein; statesmen like Disraeli, Blum and Trotsky. His real heroes were the heroes of the nation in its own land: the Judges, the Kings, the Prophets—they symbolized the fundamental strength of the people. The people must be great, and a people can be great only in their own land. The Diaspora was kind of antihistory. History itself needs to be recreated in the place where it began.

He was the first genuine Jewish statesman since the Destruction of the Second Temple, because he refused to see statesmanship solely as a function; in his eyes it was a response to the needs of history, a service demanded by the times. A statesman acquires strength, uses strength and takes account of strength, but true strength lies in actual achievement.

Ben-Gurion defined the concept of "statehood" as being the precedence of the needs of the majority over the particular needs of the individual. I believe that his concept of statehood stemmed essentially from the *Politics* of Aristotle, who wrote: "And so the State naturally takes precedence over the family and even over individual persons, since the whole necessarily takes precedence over the part."

The people take precedence over rank, and the State over the workers' organizations. He believed that it was the function of rank to provide the people with incentives for progress, and in the Histadrut, with which he had a deep personal relationship, he saw a powerful tool for the construction of the State.

A state, meaning the legally constituted framework of a people in their own land, is the only way of putting an end to exile, persecution, servility, servitude, conformism, dependence on the charity of masters, cultural assimilation or physical annihilation. Statehood is the reverse of exile.

Ben-Gurion was extremely anxious about the political aptitude of his people, their ability to live an orderly civilized life governed by law, not by pity; order, not "making do"; properly constituted elections and not the law of local oligarchs; a state that serves the whole and not the faction, the spirit of the people and not the narrow interests of one section.

He was very much afraid of cunningness, which had tended to become a habit in the social life of our people. He was worried lest the political parties see the state as a vehicle for their own interests, rather than seeing themselves as the loyal servants of the people.

It is easy to talk about statehood, but it can be extremely painful when, for example, the decision has to be taken to disband the staff of the Palmach, in the face of the united opposition of colleagues and opponents. It is very hard to defend the principle of statehood when you must give the order to open fire on a Jewish ship bringing arms to a beleaguered Israel. Ben-Gurion did not recoil from these decisions, he took them with open eyes, after weighing up the pros and cons of the deed that had to be done in the light of the circumstances and the facts as they appeared to him at the decisive moment. This is exactly where he is revealed as a great statesman. The taking of a critical decision is the soul of a statesman, and his deeds—legal bread and butter.

My first meeting with David Ben-Gurion was when I was a young man, and one day I was lucky enough to hitch a ride with him from Tel Aviv to Haifa. Even at that time Ben-Gurion was a living legend and, of course, I had hoped for the ride and the chance of talking to him. I was very excited. In those days I didn't know that Ben-Gurion was not given to idle chatter and to my great disappointment almost the entire trip passed without him uttering a single word. Only when we reached the outskirts of Haifa did he suddenly turn to me and say: "Trotsky was no statesman." To this day I do not know what brought Trotsky into Ben-Gurion's car at exactly that moment, but in my desire to continue the conversation I added: "Why?" Then Ben-Gurion got a little enthusiastic and replied: "What sort of policy is 'No peace and no war'? It is a Jewish contrivance. If it is to be peace, then one must pay the price—which is sometimes very heavy—for it. If it is to be war—then one must take the terrible risk involved. Lenin understood this. And although it may be that from an intellectual standpoint Trotsky was superior to Lenin, politically speaking Lenin understood the Russian people and this was the reason that he became their true leader."

It is impossible to stick a simple tag on Ben-Gurion. Those who try to define Ben-Gurion as a "hawk" or a "dove" have a difficult task ahead of them. In opposition to the superficially "hawkish" position, Ben-Gurion decided in favor of withdrawal; for example, withdrawal from the whole of Sinai. And in opposition to the naïvely "dovish" position, Ben-Gurion decided in favor of war; for example, war to secure the opening of the Straits of Tiran. These decisions did not arise from dogma or obsession. The deliberation that leads to decision must be fundamental, objective, responsible and cautious. Circumstances change—decisions must change too. There are times when daring is required, at other times caution is necessary.

His daring and his caution, his aptitude for decision and his rebellious instincts, his love of the truth—I was in a position to observe these things on many occasions. And three incidents are engraved especially deeply in my memory: the twenty-second

Zionist Congress; the meetings in Paris which preceded the Suez Campaign; and Ben-Gurion's meeting with De Gaulle in 1960.

The twenty-second Zionist Congress, held in Basel in December 1942, was a stormy session. This was the congress that was obliged to decide whether the State of Israel was to be established at the price of a territorial compromise, at the price of partition.

The Congress was convened to consider the "Morrison Plan" which Ben-Gurion described as "a modification of the 1939 White Paper." This plan called for the partition of Eretz Israel into four sectors, of which the smallest sector of all—the coastal strip—was to be the Jewish portion. The plan deprived Israel of the Negev and Jerusalem and, needless to say, Judaea and Samaria. It limited potential immigration to a total of 100,000 Jewish immigrants from only three countries of origin: Austria, Germany and Italy; and this right was restricted to "young artisans and agricultural workers, children and the old and infirm." According to the terms of this plan, presented by Herbert Morrison as Foreign Secretary of the Attlee Government, a Jewish–Arab committee was to meet under the auspices of the British Government and express its opinion of the scheme.

David Ben-Gurion felt that he was in a minority at the Congress. "I speak only in my own name," he declared in his address. "It may be that my views are shared by no other members of the Executive." He believed that the time had come for the pact with the British to be terminated, and in his speech to the

Congress he demanded "the establishment of a Jewish State at the very earliest opportunity." He insisted on Jewish independence, saying that "only through independence is independence to be achieved." And he was prepared to pay the price of independence: "We are willing to negotiate on the question of compromise, on this thing that is called Partition, because a Jewish State in part of Eretz Israel is preferable to a British Mandate over the whole of Eretz Israel."

Ben-Gurion believed that such a state, at a time when there existed "not a Jewish problem, but a Jewish catastrophe," would provide for us "in exchange for a limitation of our territory, greater rights over the territory that is left, rights that will permit more immigration and more settlement than in all the territory that is under British control." For this reason he was prepared to fight the British, calling for the partition of Eretz Israel as a means of procuring the immediate establishment of a Jewish State, and to fight his colleagues for an increase in unofficial immigration—"illegal immigration," as the British called it.

His speech to the Congress could be summarized in the following three demands: (1) opening the gates of Eretz Israel to Jewish immigration; (2) this immigration to be under the control of the Jewish Agency, the Agency having full authority to organize the development of the land; (3) steps to be taken toward the conversion of Eretz Israel into a Jewish State.

He was opposed by a very broad coalition

headed by Chaim Weizmann and Nahum Gold-
mann, who for different reasons were against a rift
with Britain; they were also supported by most of
the representatives of British Jewry, who had committed themselves fully to Weizmann's leadership.
Also in the opposition camp was the undisputed
leader of American Jewry, Dr. Abba Hillel Silver.
Silver's oratory was scintillating but his political
standpoint was unclear; it was impossible to tell
whether he was for or against partition, for or
against attending the London Conference, for or
against unofficial immigration. Of one thing there
was absolutely no doubt—he was totally opposed to
Ben-Gurion.

Yitzhak Tabenkin, leader of the United Kibbutz
Movement, attacked Ben-Gurion's scheme in the
most adamant terms, declaring his implacable opposition to the idea of partition. Ya'akov Hazan,
leader of Hashomer Hatzair (The Young Guard), also
deprecated Ben-Gurion's standpoint, claiming that
" 'Biltmore' is disrupting settlement."

There were also sharp divisions of opinion
within Ben-Gurion's own party. Many delegates
supported the leadership and policies of Dr. Weizmann; influential people like Eliezer Kaplan, Yosef
Sprinzak, even Moshe Sharett, made no attempt to
hide their solidarity with the man and their support
for his policy. It was clear to them, as it was to
everyone, that acceptance of Ben-Gurion's strategy
would mean the removal of Dr. Weizmann from the
leadership of the Zionist movement. Weizmann's

finest hour had been the achievement of the Balfour Declaration and the agreement with Great Britain; he was now under enormous pressure because of the demand for a break with Britain. Ben-Gurion said quite explicitly: "Eretz Israel does not belong to Britain; it is not a part of the British Empire, and the British have no right to impose their will on it."

Mapai was faced with a difficult decision. The question was debated by the party faction, which met in a basement room of the conference building. Elected to the faction for the first time were two young delegates: Moshe Dayan and myself. On the eve of the Congress we spent a lot of time in conversation, and a long-lasting friendship was formed between us. Needless to say we were both "activists" —enthusiastic supporters of Ben-Gurion.

We arrived at the Congress with firm views and with great curiosity, eager to see for the first time how decisions were taken in the highest Zionist institution. Naturally we looked around for people who shared our views. It was at this time that I became a friend of Arieh Bahir, a leading member of Kibbutz Afikim, a community renowned for its bold, uncompromising and unwavering support for Ben-Gurion. The association with Afikim was very precious to Ben-Gurion, and he regarded Arieh Bahir as a man worthy of total trust, a man to be relied on in all circumstances.

I arrived with Arieh in the basement room where the party faction had been convened, and we waited for the meeting to begin. We were somewhat surprised when Ben-Gurion, in spite of his reputation for punctuality, failed to arrive at the appointed time. Suddenly Paula Ben-Gurion arrived, in a state of great agitation and fury. She approached Arieh Bahir and said, gasping for breath: "He's gone mad —again!" It was clear who she was talking about. Arieh's response was just as brief: "Where is he?" "In the hotel," said Paula.

Arieh turned to me: "Come on, let's go."

We left the Congress Building and made our way to the Drei Königen Hotel, where Herzl had stayed during the earliest congresses. We climbed the stairs to Ben-Gurion's room and rang the bell; there was no reply. The door was not locked; Arieh opened it and we went inside. We were amazed at what we saw: Ben-Gurion standing at the table in the middle of the room, packing his suitcase.

We said, almost in chorus: "Shalom, Ben-Gurion." He did not reply. After a few minutes he turned to face us. His expression was grave and tense. Without responding to our greeting he said: "Are you coming with me?"

Arieh replied boldly: "Yes, but where are you going?"

"I am going to form a new Zionist movement. Nothing will come of this Congress. The leaders are paralyzed by fear and inertia. The delegates hate the idea of facing trouble and they are ready to agree to anything, at a time when our people should be swimming against the tide, struggling and fighting, daring to challenge the old order! In this Congress

there is a solid majority behind Weizmann, support-
ing his acceptance of a bad reality. There is a majority here in favor of surrendering to the Morrison
Plan, a scheme that will kill immigration and put an
end to all our Zionist aspirations. This Congress will
vote for the destruction of our future! Our people
need a new movement, a movement of committed
young pioneers. I shall go to them and I shall go with
them. And we shall do what really needs to be done,
even if I am in a minority of one."

This was a stunning blow. But Arieh was of naturally calm temperament and he did not lose his
composure. He turned to Ben-Gurion and said: "You
are not alone. You may even have a majority in the
Party faction. . . ."

Ben-Gurion interrupted him brusquely: "We
don't have majority in the Party faction."

But Arieh went on unperturbed: "We, Shimon
and I, will go with you. And many of our colleagues
will do the same. But first of all we must find out
whether we have a majority or not."

"That will take time."

"Perhaps you're right. But we can set a time
limit on our inquiries."

"How long?" asked Ben-Gurion.

"Till tomorrow morning," replied Arieh. Then
he added: "The Party faction is already in session
and waiting for you to arrive." Ben-Gurion put down
his suitcase and said: "Let's go."

Meanwhile news had reached the Party faction,
perhaps through Paula, that a crisis had arisen.

Many of those who wanted Weizmann to stay did not want Ben-Gurion to go; they would have preferred them both to stay.

Golda Meir took the chair. Once more she appeared at her best—and most determined. The atmosphere was electric; the tension was almost physically perceptible. Golda demanded that there be no heckling. In spite of her opposition to the idea of partition, she threw her support behind Ben-Gurion. When we arrived, Ben-Gurion was given the floor.

He began with an attack on Eliezer Kaplan, whom on this occasion he called "Engineer Kaplan" (a reference to his mechanical approach to the subject). Then he said that the Zionist movement had always espoused the cause of the establishment of a Jewish State. Now the time had come to unfurl the flag of statehood—it was inevitable. He, Ben-Gurion, was in favor of "compromise," because the alternative was "partition without a state," a partition that would be enforced by the British and would stifle immigration and settlement. It was unthinkable that control of settlement and immigration be handed over to the British. There were those who were so much in love with Britain that they forgot the reasons for which we had gone along with the British; now that the British had broken their promise, there was no longer any point in cooperating with them.

Ben-Gurion attacked some of his colleagues on the grounds that their position was incomprehensible; it was impossible to tell if they were for or against partition, for or against participating in a London Conference, for an increase in unofficial immigration or prepared to accept restrictions. He despised those who were committed to the mandatory principle to the extent that they were ready to hand over the Mandate to another state, to *any* state, "seeing that one delegate has suggested that the Mandate be given to Mussolini and others have suggested that it be offered to Poland."

Ben-Gurion demanded an immediate, firm and clear decision, since "a Jewish State is no longer a final objective; it is a feasible demand."

Eliezer Kaplan rose to reply. His tone was no less acerbic. He nicknamed his opponent "Advocate Ben-Gurion" (a reference to his instinct for controversy). He claimed that we had lost nothing through our ties with Great Britain. Under her Mandate we had brought in immigrants and established settlements; we had gained international respect and a break with Britain would hurt us more than her. We had built up the land through a policy of constant self-restraint, he said, but we had defended ourselves when the need arose; this policy suited our character and did not conflict with our interests.

The stormy debate lasted into the small hours of the morning. Finally a vote was taken: the majority, though by no means large, was in support of Ben-Gurion.

Victory in the party faction assured us of victory in the Congress. It confirmed the legitimacy of the demand for the establishment of the State, at the price of partition of the country and a break with Britain. A new page was turned in the history of Zionism. The minority of one had become a majority, a majority that had set out upon a new path. The seed was sown and the first step taken toward the creation of the Jewish State—the greatest of all Ben-Gurion's great achievements.

Ten years later, in October 1956, I was witness to another scene. Ben-Gurion announced that in his view the Egyptian blockade of the Straits of Tiran constituted a *causus belli*. As early as December 1955 he was prepared to send an expeditionary force of the Israeli Army to occupy the entire coastline of the Gulf, from Eilat to Sharm-El-Sheikh, and to lift the blockade of the Straits, by force if necessary. He believed that from the point of view of settlement the Negev was the area of the greatest potential for the future of Israel. At the twenty-second Congress he had told us an anecdote concerning the two Socialist philosophers Dr. Chaim Jitlowsky and Nahman Sirkin. One day Sirkin said to Jitlowsky: "Let's divide up the Jewish world between us. You take all that there is, and I'll take everything that is missing. The Diaspora exists—you can have it. There is no Eretz Israel—I shall take that."

The nonexistent Eretz Israel, the uninhabited Eretz Israel, Eretz Israel the reverse of the Diaspora —this was what the Negev meant to Ben-Gurion. As he said some time later to the French president, General De Gaulle: "The real meaning of the Cold

War is a struggle for the souls of the peoples of Africa and Asia, who are waking up to the idea of independence and will exert a decisive influence on the future of the world." He believed that Eilat was Israel's gateway to the peoples of Africa and Asia, a vital communications route that must not be in any way endangered.

There were two reasons for which war seemed imminent: one was the blockade of the Straits of Tiran; the other was the increase in acts of terrorism mounted from the Gaza Strip and Jordan. Israel was compelled to respond firmly, and only a short step separated terrorism and reprisal from the outbreak of full-scale war.

At this time, in my capacity as Director of the Ministry of Defense, I initiated and developed our relations with France. In the course of an official visit to Paris I heard from the French leaders about "Operation Musketeer," the Anglo–French operation whose object was to guarantee, by military force, the renewal of international sovereignty over the Suez Canal, which Nasser had nationalized. Naturally we took an increasing interest in the possibility of joint action, if not in the objectives of the war, then at least in its timing. Any state that is faced with the danger of war wishes to meet it under the least dangerous conditions.

Ben-Gurion trusted the sincerity of France, but he was suspicious of Britain's intentions. He saw Eden as the founder and patron of the Arab League and believed that the Anglo–Jordanian pact would

one day work against Israel. It came to him as no
surprise when, after the punitive raid against Kalki-
lia, on October 12, 1956, the British representative,
Mr. Westlook, knocked on his door early in the
morning and informed him that an Iraqi division
would be entering Jordan in three days' time (two
weeks before the Suez Operation!). Westlook added
that Britain was bound by agreements to Iraq and to
Jordan, and would tolerate no interference with this
troop movement. This episode only confirmed Ben-
Gurion's suspicion that these agreements were designed to threaten Israel's security.

In the negotiations between ourselves and the
French I took no decisions without Ben-Gurion's au-
thorization, and yet I was not entirely sure what his
ultimate and decisive reaction would be regarding
the outcome; he was very careful not to commit
himself prematurely and until the time was ripe he
would not show his hand, even to his closest aides.
But I knew that if Israel were to undertake any military operation in collaboration with the French and
the British, this would be done only if the following
preconditions were guaranteed:

(a) Any cooperation must be that of equal partners. Israel would not accept the status of a junior
partner, even in regard to major powers like Britain
and France.

(b) Israel would not agree to being "a sword for
hire." She was prepared to endanger herself only for
the sake of defined objectives in her own interests.

(c) Ben-Gurion would not consent to any operation that would allow freedom of maneuver to Britain; he feared that Britain was liable to turn against us at the last moment.

(d) The bombing of civilian targets, either in Egypt or Israel, was a risk that he was not prepared to accept.

When Guy Mollet, the French Prime Minister, invited him to visit France in the second half of October 1956, Ben-Gurion was constantly asking me if Mollet knew that he, Ben-Gurion, had committed himself to no partnership whatsoever, either with the British or the French.

A special plane, the plane that had been a personal gift to De Gaulle from President Roosevelt, was sent to fly us to Paris. Since the journey was secret, we took off from a military airbase, arriving there in a small civilian car with the blinds pulled down. Crowded into the car were Ben-Gurion, Moshe Dayan, Nehemiah Argov and myself. We were accompanied on the flight by a representative of the French Defense Ministry, Louis Mangin, and Israel's representatives in Paris, Yosef Nehemias and Asher Ben-Natan. On the way to the airbase Ben-Gurion explained to us that he accepted Guy Mollet's invitation only because he did not want to upset Franco–Israeli relations. When Nehemiah commented that they would put "definitive terms" to us, Ben-Gurion said: "In that case, we shall go home immediately."

At Sèvres, near Paris, we met Guy Mollet, the Minister of Defense, Maurice Bourgès-Maunoury, and Foreign Minister Christian Pineau. Ben-Gurion spoke first of the need to redraw the map of the Middle East. Among other things, he was afraid that the Sykes-Picot Agreement, signed during the First World War, had given too much territory to the part of Lebanon which was inhabited by Muslims, and thus endangered the future of Lebanon as a Christian state. Beyond this he spoke only on philosophical and philological topics; it was impossible to bring him to more concrete deliberation—this he left to us.

From the information that we supplied, he became convinced that his anxieties were well-founded; the British were prepared to cooperate with the French; as for Israel, they wanted her to provide the pretext—we should put our chestnuts into the fire, and then the British could intervene to separate the so-called aggressors: Egypt and Israel. We insisted that this was quite out of the question.

In the formal negotiations, and also in the private behind-the-scenes talks that we held with our French allies, we made it absolutely clear to them that Ben-Gurion had not yet committed himself to *anything,* and that there was no prospect of inducing him to come to an agreement, unless it was to be full tripartite cooperation between equal partners. The French worked very hard at persuading the British that without the acceptance of this condition, no agreement with Israel could be secured.

Toward the end of the Sèvres Conference, a British representative finally appeared, Foreign Secretary Selwyn Lloyd, accompanied by two senior government officials; only then did Ben-Gurion agree to take an active part in the negotiations. He emphasized most adamantly that the project under discussion was coordination of *timing*, not of operations, and that even in this case we should honor Churchill's principle, laid down during the Second World War, that partnership between allied armies should be bound up with the independent political objectives of the warring nations.

The British were still looking for a "pretext" for the operation. And in an effort to facilitate British participation in the scheme, one of the French negotiators, General Challe, made the following suggestion: Israel would announce that one of her cities had been bombed, and then she would go to war; an Anglo–French force would then intervene, ostensibly to impose a cease-fire. This proposal brought the Sèvres Conference to a dramatic climax—and came close to wrecking it altogether.

As General Challe went on to explain the advantages of his "scenario," we could see the anger growing on Ben-Gurion's face, like a tightly-pressed spring about to break loose. His expression stern, his voice clear and hard, Ben-Gurion asked Ben-Natan to translate his words "sentence by sentence." And his reply was roughly as follows:

"I wish to say something irrational and possibly naïve. Moreover, I want to speak not in my capacity as Prime Minister, but as an Israeli citizen. Israel is strong because she has a reason for fighting, because she is fighting for justice. I—I am not capable of lying, not to world public opinion nor to anyone else. I will accept no plan that forces us to lie."

With that we were on the point of withdrawing from the talks, and had it not been that one of the engines of our plane was in need of repair, we would certainly have returned home there and then.

Ben-Gurion's firm stand, the determination of the French to arrive at an honorable partnership in spite of the obstacles, the change in Britain's attitude—a change brought about partly by Ben-Gurion's firmness and partly by the results of the Jordanian elections (which had produced a coalition favoring an armed alliance of Jordan, Syria and Egypt)—all of these factors brought the negotiations to a point where agreement seemed possible.

The time had come for the Prime Minister of Israel to make his decision. Ben-Gurion had not yet revealed to anyone—not even to us—what his final position would be. He simply did not want to make his views known, perhaps not even to finalize them in his own mind, until satisfactory preconditions had been obtained.

He did not want to haggle—he left that to us— nor did he want to adopt a position likely to deprive Israel of the opportunity to arrive at free and independent decisions. As for committing himself, he left that to the last possible moment. The time had now come. On October 24, two days after the beginning of the conference, the telephone rang in our Paris hotel, and Ben-Gurion invited Moshe Dayan and myself to join him at Sèvres. The conference had been adjourned that morning, for separate talks between the French and the British. We arrived at the villa in Sèvres and found Ben-Gurion and Nehemiah Argov sitting in the garden. It was a sunny autumn day, and the air was very clear. Ben-Gurion was surprised to see us arriving so soon.

Ben-Gurion asked Dayan to draw him a sketch of the plan of the operation; we had no map with us, so I took out a cigarette packet and Dayan drew a map of Sinai on the back of it, with three arrows pointing west in the center of the peninsula.

Ben-Gurion had prepared a list of ten questions. The purpose of these questions was to make it clear that we had, and would have, no interest in territorial expansion, except perhaps for a corridor connecting Eilat with Sharm-el-Sheikh, if this proved to be the only means of guaranteeing our freedom of navigation in the Gulf. Then we knew that his mind was made up; after a sleepless night he had finally arrived at a decision.

The experienced leader was once more in control. The State of Israel had been established under his guidance, the War of Independence won under his leadership. Now once more he was taking a risk for the sake of our future security—opening the way to Africa and Asia, and putting an end to the activities of terrorist infiltrators.

These two decisions—in favor of war and in favor of withdrawal—were taken by him in conditions of total isolation; all eyes were on him and it was his duty to decide. I once asked Ben-Gurion when he first felt himself a leader. He preferred to be called "the one responsible," and he answered my question as follows:

"I first felt responsible when I realized that I had nobody to ask and that the decision was mine alone; then I knew that the moment had arrived."

Another memorable incident occurred during Ben-Gurion's visit to Paris in June 1960. We dined with General De Gaulle at the Elysée Palace, and after the meal the General showed Ben-Gurion the magnificent gardens of the Palace. ("When shall we have gardens such as these?" Ben-Gurion asked as the television cameramen swarmed around him.) I walked behind the two statesmen; they made a strange looking pair: one with his distinctive height and the other with his distinctive mane of hair—two great warriors who seemed to have found a common tongue.

In the garden there were tables and chairs. Charles De Gaulle, Ben-Gurion and Debrais (the French Prime Minister) sat down at the first table. De Gaulle invited me to join them, saying with a thin smile: "I am sure that you know Paris well—its sights and its treasures, political and physical." Then he turned to Ben-Gurion and said: "Tell me, what are your true aspirations regarding the frontiers of Israel? Tell me and I promise it will be kept secret. I know that your country is small. Do you want the mountains to the east, or the desert in the south?"

Ben-Gurion admired De Gaulle very much and he blushed like a little boy, greatly moved. Then a broad smile spread over his face and he replied without hesitating: "If you had asked me that question fifteen years ago I would have given the following answer: I should like the State of Israel to include the mountains of Transjordan and the river Litani." General De Gaulle had once served in the Lebanon and he repeated the name "Litani" as if he suddenly understood the significance of a mysterious dream. "But since you ask me today," Ben-Gurion continued, "I shall tell you, with all sincerity, that I am more concerned with the problems of immigration and peace than with the question of territory. I am prepared to be content with the existing frontiers, so long as we can achieve peace and bring in more Jews."

De Gaulle looked surprised: "What, more Jews?"

"Yes," replied Ben-Gurion. "Today we have in Israel a total of two million Jews; Israel does not exist only for them. We want to double this number, both to save the Jewish people and to strengthen the State of Israel."

De Gaulle wanted to know where the Jews would come from, and Ben-Gurion explained to him that they would come from all four corners of the world, from both America and Russia. Suddenly De Gaulle stood up and told one of his aides to summon Couve de Murville, the Foreign Minister, and Guy Mollet, who were sitting at a nearby table. They both came and joined us. When they had sat down De Gaulle turned to them with a mischievous grin and said: "President Ben-Gurion wants more Jews. He's only got two million Jews. That isn't enough for him. He wants settlers more than he wants land. He's dreaming of a people, not of territory."

Seven years later De Gaulle made a speech accusing the Jewish people of arrogance and territorial greed. This speech offended Ben-Gurion deeply. (He was then a private citizen in Sdeh Boker, his kibbutz in the Negev.) He asked me if I could recall any occasion on which De Gaulle might have gained the impression, even indirectly, that we were interested in territorial expansion. I reminded Ben-Gurion of the conversation in the gardens of the Elysée, but on that occasion, uncharacteristically, he had made no record of the conversation. I told him that I had jotted down the main points of what had been said in my diary. At his request I showed him these extracts, and in the detailed letter that he sent to De Gaulle in reply, Ben-Gurion quoted from my diary. De Gaulle's response was self-righteous; he claimed that he had not intended to censure the Jewish people at all, and that the national characteristics to which he referred in his speech were not negative as such.

I saw Ben-Gurion deciding in favor of war, which always involves risk, and in favor of withdrawal, which can be very painful, especially when it means giving up a part of one's homeland. But as early as the twenty-second Zionist Congress he had spoken in favor of partition as the price for the establishment of a Jewish State, to which Jews could come at once and in large numbers; and in his conversation with De Gaulle, sixteen years later, he made it clear that immigration was of greater concern to him than territory.

Ben-Gurion took important decisions; they were accompanied by equally important achievements. The first major task that he performed in the cause of statehood, a task undertaken with extraordinary enthusiasm, the enthusiasm of a lover, was the creation of the IDF (Israel Defense Forces). In the progress of the IDF he invested all his faith in Jewish statehood. It was to be a people's army; an army without factions; an army divorced from party politics; an army whose officers are chosen for their merit and ability, but not an army in which service is made into a career; an army alive with the pioneering spirit; an army ruled by law, discipline, knowledge, truth and comradeship. Ben-Gurion molded the IDF and the younger generation at a single stroke. To the higher ranks he appointed young men who in the course of time earned the public's respect. He described himself as a man who "had the great privilege of representing civilian authority in the army." He took a detailed interest in everything that concerned the IDF. He saw the commanders as his friends and he felt a deep personal affinity with them. He believed in them and from them he demanded moderation, humility and discipline. He gave them ample scope for initiative and independence; he encouraged them to spread their wings and fly high and far, exploring new dimensions of strategy and leadership.

He saw the army as "a melting-pot for the nation," a school for the people, a place for the acquisition of correct Hebrew, love of the land, loyalty to the people, professional innovation going hand in hand with pioneering leadership—the workshop and refinery of an ancient and a new people. He looked forward to the day when a Jew from Yemen would be appointed Chief of Staff. He insisted that all officers adopt Hebrew names, so that the new Jewish history should know its heroes by Hebrew, not foreign names. He esteemed military daring very highly and he respected the courageous officer who marches at the head of his troops and sets them a good example.

Ben-Gurion took an interest in the army's operations and its structures, in equipment and in military research, but in general he relied on the men who worked on his behalf; his influence was like that of a wind, ever-present and all-pervading. But when the need arose to come to a decision on a particular issue, he was not content with general guidance; he rolled up his sleeves and applied himself to the most minute details of the problem.

He was keen to develop the links between the people and the IDF. From the army he demanded loyalty to the people; from the people he demanded affection for the army. He resisted all attempts at involving the army in political debate. As Minister of Defense he saw himself as the representative of the entire Government, not as the envoy of a single party. Above all else he saw himself as responsible to the mothers and fathers of serving soldiers. The lot of bereaved families was his constant concern. In his preface to the anthology *Scrolls of Fire,* edited by Reuven Avinoam, Ben-Gurion wrote the following dedication: "To Reuven, who lost his son and found his generation." Through the writings of the sons and the sufferings of the families he learned to appreciate afresh the human richness stored within our people and the human tragedy inherent in the untimely loss of some of its finest sons.

Ben-Gurion toyed with the idea of earning a paratrooper's wings. But Moshe Dayan, then Chief of Staff, told him: "If you wish to volunteer for the IDF, you will have to obey orders, and I order you to concentrate on your job as Minister of Defense."

As Minister of Defense he looked to the future with great anxiety. On December 17, 1956, after the Suez Campaign, he addressed a conference of senior officers and said: "It may be that in the next war we shall not be the ones to take the initiative but will face the initiative taken by others; it is extremely likely that we shall be attacked not by one army but by several. The Egyptians of today are not the same as the Egyptians of eight years ago. So let us not underestimate the severity of the next encounter."

Ben-Gurion saw the concept of security as a concentrated effort involving various factors. When the Ministry of Defense was first established, a number of different names were proposed for it: "Ministry of Defense," "Ministry of War," "Army Ministry"; but he preferred "Ministry of Security," because: "The security of Israel implies immigration, and it means settlement; security includes control of the sea and of the air, having a strong navy and air force; security is the development of scientific research and scientific aptitude in all disciplines—physics, chemistry, biology and advanced technology; the security of Israel is the mobilization of our youth and the involvement of the people and its scholars in the pursuit of difficult and vital objectives—settlement, defense and integration of the exiles."

Security is not a limited function but multiple effort; it is like a high-tension cable, concentrating national energy and using it to reinforce the nation's ability to survive. It is both existing energy and potential energy. Ben-Gurion saw this potential as consisting in scientific and technological development. "Scientific research and its achievements," he wrote, "are no longer simply an abstract, intellectual business, essentially supplying the spiritual and scholarly needs of a few initiates, but a factor of central importance to our everyday lives, a factor which—together with the sweat of our hands—is the first and fundamental condition for the progress of a cultured people."

In the field of science he insisted that we be forward looking, and not complacent. "Experts know only what has happened in the past; no expert can tell with certainty what the future will bring." But the past and the present are by nature of limited scope; our territory is small and our people few. That which lies in the future—the new scientific potential—can break down our natural barriers and open up before us a world of new possibilities.

Traditional strategy depends on the utilization of three basic elements: time, space and quantity. But science and technology challenge these elements. An aircraft that flies faster than the speed of sound undermines the concept of time; a missile traveling through the stratosphere, over mountains and deserts and seas, undermines the concept of space; the splitting of the atom, releasing vast energy and creating new energy, undermines the concept of quantity.

It has been the fate of Israel to be born into a world where the level of progress is in competition with the accepted norms of physics. Of course we must take care that time is not wasted, that space is conserved, that quantities are increased; but it is our duty to take advantage of these new possibilities and ensure that the next generation of Jewish security is a generation founded on new qualities, in mind and material, so that we may be both stronger and more independent.

It was with these considerations in mind that we laid the foundations of an aircraft industry. The question was asked: how can a state that is not yet capable of manufacturing cars embark on the manufacture of jet aircraft? Only a handful of states are equipped to cope with this industry, in which the risks are enormous, the technology new and the investment high. But Ben-Gurion stood firm. "What America can do in the industrial field must be our objective too."

With Ben-Gurion we dreamed of harnessing atomic power for research purposes and, in the future, for the generation of electricity and the desalination of sea water, and what then seemed distant and extravagant and implausible, is seen today as natural and indispensable. This also applies to missiles. "Not a penny spent on missiles" was a slogan widely heard. But we persisted, again with Ben-Gurion's support, and this persistence has paid off today in the shape of such achievements in military hardware as the surface-to-surface missile Gabriel, and the air-to-air missile Shafrir.

Ben-Gurion sniffed the scent of gunpowder in these debates. But he did not hesitate to make decisions. When I came to him with a plan costing, for example, ten thousand Israeli pounds, Ben-Gurion would ask with a groan: "Where would we find the money for that?" If, on the other hand, I put forward a plan costing ten million, he would comment, quite seriously, that this was not an excessive sum. His meaning was clear: that which is not essential is expensive even when it is cheap; but the essential is reasonably priced whatever its cost. It is the leader's responsibility to make decisions according to value, not price.

Science appealed greatly to Ben-Gurion's imagination. But technological advance was not his only preoccupation. He knew that while improving our defensive capability we must also lay the foundations of a future in which Israel might live in security and on peaceful terms with her neighbors. "The fate of Israel," he said, "depends on two things: her strength and her justice." Ben-Gurion devoted great efforts to the objective of making peace—"a true peace"—with the Arab States. He valued the contacts that were made with King Abdullah of Jordan during the War of Independence. He tried to negotiate with Nasser. After the Six Day War, when he heard that Mussa Alami, the Arab leader from Jericho, was in London, he flew to Britain for the specific purpose of renewing the talks that had been interrupted by the course of events.

He hoped that Israel would be a nation contributing to the progress of liberated and developing countries. He asked Moshe Sharett to go to Burma immediately after its independence, to attend the Socialist Congress that had been convened there and to investigate the prospects of establishing links with that country. He took a great interest in what we were doing to help Burma. He read the memoirs of the leader of the Ghanaian independence movement, Kwame Nkrumah, and sent envoys to Ghana with offers of aid. He sought to establish relations with Ethiopia, Iran and Turkey, and although he used to say, "It doesn't matter what the other nations say, what matters is what the Jews do," he tried hard to create an atmosphere of trust between

Israel and the other nations of the world. He used to prepare meticulously for his talks with heads of state in the United States, Britain and France, and whenever he told them anything, or made them a promise, he made sure that it was fulfilled to the letter. Proud Jew that he was, he was also a responsible citizen of the international community. "America is making a grave mistake in not seeking relations with China," he wrote, "since there is no practical conflict of interests between the United States and China." He explained this view in a letter to the late President Kennedy. To De Gaulle he offered advice on how to deal with the Algerian problem. His political interests did indeed embrace the whole world.

Security, science, statesmanship and settlement —these were the factors that he believed would do justice to the Jewish people. He once described the objective of Israel's foreign policy as follows: "It is a policy aimed at establishing links with every state in which Jews live, so that the Jews who live there can maintain their links with Israel." Similarly, the aim of Ben-Gurion's domestic policy was to create a state to which Jews would be able, willing and eager to immigrate.

In my diary I have found an extract from remarks made to me by Ben-Gurion in October 1967:

> I don't know how many children in Israel have had fathers as wonderful as mine was—a Zionist, a member of the "Lovers of

Zion" fraternity, an intellectual. But once I arrived in Eretz Israel, I found myself asking a pertinent question: why, in fact, did he not come here? What is Zionism? Is it only a belief? I must go back to Sdeh Boker. I must finish my writings. Our young people should be told about the heroic deeds that laid the foundations of the State of Israel. Dr. Hissin, for example, traveled to Eretz Israel on foot. What led him to make this journey? How did he conceive the great idea of building *villages* in Eretz Israel?

He had no doubt that the Jews of Russia would come, that the Jews of America would come, that the Jews of South Africa would come. He knew that his was a stubborn people, but he also believed it was a great people, whose future would not fail the expectation of its past.

In another conversation Ben-Gurion said to me: "Of all the men who came to Israel in the Second Aliyah, the most remarkable were Shlomo Lavie and Ben-Zion Yisraeli. Lavie never complained. When his wife died, his wife whom he dearly loved, he did not say a word. His two sons fell in the War of Independence; he said nothing. He suffered terribly, but in silence. In spite of all these tragedies he was steadfast in his faith and he was a great pioneer, a fine son of a wonderful race. You know," he added, "in fact Lavie was not a farmer originally; he began as a worker in the factory at Lod. Yes, agriculture, industry and faith . . ." and Ben-Gurion's eyes filled with tears.

At the end of his life as at the beginning, he was fascinated by the primeval state. The stubborn old visionary retired to the seclusion of a wooden shack in Sdeh Boker, "a landscape untouched by the hand of politics," as Alterman described it.

In the last decade of his life the "Lavon Affair" brought him into conflict with the prevailing mood of public opinion and with the majority of his colleagues. I am convinced that Ben-Gurion saw the issue in moral, not political terms. "The truth takes precedence over everything," he wrote in his account of the business. He claimed that it was illegal for ministers to act as judges; truth takes no account of rank and accords no preferential treatment.

As a result of the "Affair" he resigned from Mapai, the party which he had created, and formed a breakaway group—Rafi, the "Israeli Workers' List." A number of enthusiastic young people rallied around the new party, but it won only ten seats in the Knesset in the 1965 elections.

He suffered a further blow when on the eve of the Six Day War Rafi decided, against his advice, to join a government of national unity.

He prophesied that one day we would be attacked by the Arabs—and taken by surprise. It was as if he had clear foreknowledge of the Yom Kippur War.

Concern for the fate of the people, his self-imposed ostracism from political life, his deteriorating health—all of these were a constant burden to him.

He reckoned that he would die at the age of eighty-six or eighty-seven, the average life span of his forebears. For this reason he worked on his memoirs from sunrise to sunset, anxious to pass on his experience to his successors.

He saw old age approaching. He contemplated his end without cowardice and without delusions. He retained his extraordinary personal charm. He never complained, he never asked favors, and he never stopped hoping. He hoped that Sdeh Boker, where he asked to be buried, would become the cultural, academic and scientific center of a progressive Israel.

In January 1968 his wife Paula died. She had cared for him in an almost maternal fashion, making sure that he ate suitable meals, rested at regular intervals, was not bothered by too many visitors, and received proper medical treatment (she was a qualified nurse). She was also constantly advising him about people, because she thought him a poor judge of character.

When the news of her death became known, I received a call from Chaim Israeli, and we traveled together to the hospital in Beersheba. There we found Ben-Gurion sitting in a chair, wrapped up in himself and saying nothing. He had known for some time that Paula was close to the end, and her death did not come as a shock to him. He glanced at us, smiled and said: "Let's go to Sdeh Boker." He drove us there in his car, and we traveled in silence until we reached the door of his shack.

In his study, he said that he needed to drink

something. We found a bottle and glasses, and Ben-Gurion began to reveal a little of what was going on in his mind. He said: "Twice she followed me. The first time—to Eretz Israel, although she knew no Hebrew and she already had a young child. And the second time—here, to the desert, to isolation. She left behind all her friends and the life that she had grown accustomed to, and came here. I made only one mistake, where she was concerned. I was sure that she would outlive me, and she has died before me. There is no escaping from death, nor is there any reason to be afraid of it. It is inevitable. The question is how we live, not how we die."

Five years later, on a Sabbath morning in December 1973, Chaim Israeli called me on the telephone. He said one word: "Ben-Gurion." The room was filled with a strange sense: a nation orphaned.

I hurried to the hospital in Tel-Hashomer. Members of his family, his sons and sons-in-law, were waiting outside. I asked permission to go into the little room. He lay there motionless, his massive forehead, pale as a marble slab, framed by his mane of white hair. I sensed that for the first time since his birth, he was truly, finally, at rest. A rare phenomenon of nature, submitting to a law of nature from which there is no escaping.

Ben-Gurion's appearance on the stage of Jewish history came about at a fateful hour for our people. They were a people accustomed to disaster; he was a man accustomed to faith. He transcended the disaster of his people and inspired them with his extraordinary faith, he gave them a new security, a creative pride. He conquered their despair, aroused their dynamic instinct and appealed to their latent heroism; he demanded of them hard work and determination and justice. He led them in their wars, he fought their negative habits. He guided and consoled, warned and encouraged, he told the truth and he told of his visions. His arm was strong and his soul was pure. But above all else he embodied the spirit of the Jewish people: a great and obstinate spirit, a rebellious and stormy spirit, a spirit that challenges the rules of Creation, a believing and creative spirit. And David Ben-Gurion, alone of his generation, not only symbolized this spirit, he was its guide. The wind blew and he maintained its strength; he gave it direction and he rose with it to the heights where the past and the future meet again, where the vast perspectives do not diminish mankind but endow him with new energy and the will to fight.

In might and in spirit. He stood up to both. He distinguished between them. And through them he taught us that the time for satisfaction had not yet arrived; that we still had a long way to go, and that if we spread the sails with care, the wind of his spirit would continue to fill them, guiding us on toward the new dawn of the Jewish nation.

LEVI ESHKOL
A Wise Balance

In a place where there is no man, Nature is sterile.

WILLIAM BLAKE

"THE INSCRIPTION on my tombstone will be: 'Here lies a man who had great prospects,' " Levi Eshkol once joked when I visited him on the eve of the War of Independence, to tell him that Ben-Gurion wanted him as Deputy Minister of Defense.

Eshkol had a wonderful sense of humor. Moreover, he did not even spare himself as a butt for his own sarcasm. In this, as in many other respects, he stood apart from the other leaders of our movement. He was determined, but not obstinate, flexible, but not submissive, serious in action, but humorous in speech. He did not reveal everything that he knew

—he kept back reserves of knowledge and expertise in readiness for emergencies.

He understood the art of compromise, of give and take, as means of avoiding resentment and schism, and he suspected that without compromise life is impossible: "Everybody is in love with his own compromise."

He loved to be in the center, but he was never jealous of the success or centrality of others. Rising stars did not worry him, he saw them as a sign of the enrichment of life, and not as a threat to his position. *"Junger mann,"* he used to say, "if you want to jump into the sea—jump. If you drown, we shall mourn you. If you survive—we shall meet again."

He relied on the experience of the past, but was open to every new experience. His wonderful humor was so sprightly and wise that it ceased to be pleasantry for its own sake and became a tool to be employed.

I had the good fortune to work with him for many years. It was a fluctuating experience, with many ups and downs, but even in the hardest moments it was quite free of rancor. And in both good times and bad, healthy common sense overcame personal grudge. He despised arrogance. He saw life as a constant human experiment from which there is no escape. Even after he became Prime Minister, he remained true to his ways, losing nothing of his personal warmth—it guided his every move. I shall never forget the day that he was appointed Prime Minister. He was in his office on the second floor of a small house in the Hakirya in Tel Aviv (the building where the Cabinet used to meet in the early days of the State) and I was on the ground floor of the same house, in a room that was just as large, or as small, as the Prime Minister's (I was then Deputy Minister of Defense). There was a direct telephone link between the two offices.

Suddenly I heard the telephone ring: *"Junger mann,* is that you? Well then, come upstairs for a moment." And there the following conversation took place:

ESHKOL: Do you know what I am?

I: Yes.

ESHKOL: Well then, what am I?

I: Prime Minister.

ESHKOL: Very nice, and what does a Prime Minister do?

I: A lot of important things.

ESHKOL: Yes, but what's the first, most important thing? (*Silence*)

ESHKOL: All right, I'll tell you: he makes a speech.

I: That's true.

ESHKOL: But he doesn't write the speech, it's written for him.

I: ?

ESHKOL: *Junger mann,* make a draft.

It was the custom in those days for the Prime Minister to offer to meet the President of Egypt "face to face, at any time and in any place." I prepared a draft which contained the usual offer. Eshkol looked at the draft and read it aloud, with some comments of his own (his annotations are in brackets), as follows:

"I, Prime Minister of Israel (Levi son of Deborah) Eshkol, invite the President of Egypt, Gamal Abdul Nasser (what's his mother's name?), to meet me face to face, at any time and in any place. . . ." Here Eshkol paused, turned to me and said in Yiddish: *"Junger mann, du meinst es ernst?* [Young man, are you serious?] Supposing he agrees—what shall we say to him? Have you got a plan? The meeting would be to discuss peace, and for peace you need a plan. Are you sending me off to a meeting without giving me a plan?"

This mixture of Yiddish and Hebrew, of humor and gravity, accompanied him wherever he went. He was always inquisitive, constantly asking questions, sometimes simple questions, sometimes very perceptive ones, but always without pretense or condescension.

I remember three official missions on which I accompanied him: two of them open, and one secret.

In 1964 Eshkol visited France. This was during the "honeymoon" period between ourselves and the French. He was very excited at the prospect of meeting De Gaulle. He asked me all kinds of questions about the personality of De Gaulle, his views, his attitude toward Israel. He read all the available material about the French leader and rehearsed to himself what he would say to him. As we left the Elysée Palace, Eshkol sighed with relief. The meeting had been a success. De Gaulle was impressed by Eshkol's warm personality, his charm, his down-to-earth manner. At the end of the meeting he made Eshkol a number of warm declarations of friendship.

But there were other French officials whom he was obliged to meet—Prime Minister Pompidou, Foreign Minister Couve de Murville, and Defense Minister Pierre Mesmer. Before each of these meetings Eshkol would turn to me and say in Yiddish: *"Was will ich sagen dem Sheigetz!"* * (What shall I say to the fellow?)

With Pierre Mesmer there was no problem. It is true that Mesmer spoke only French, and Eshkol's French was rather shaky, but he had planned the conversation in advance: start with the man's name and leave the question of arms to the end. . . .

The idea of discussing the name occurred to him because of the English expression "to mesmerize" (Eshkol repeatedly astonished us with his knowledge of other languages), an expression derived from the name of the Austrian hypnotist, Dr. Mesmer. Eshkol decided to see if there was a connection between the two Mesmers, and in the course of the conversation it emerged that there was. After that he presented our arms list. The meeting passed off smoothly.

He was not particularly worried about meeting Couve de Murville either. Firstly, this Frenchman spoke English; secondly, there was no shortage of foreign policy questions to discuss, ranging from our

---

* *Sheigetz* is a Yiddish term for a non-Jew.

activities in Africa to the question of our joining the European Common Market. This meeting passed smoothly as well.

But before the meeting with Pompidou Eshkol was extremely anxious. Pompidou did not speak English, and the discussions with him were not limited to issues of foreign policy or defense. On the way to the Hotel Matignon* Eshkol repeated his usual question, but this time with more emphasis: *"Was will ich sagen dem greisen Sheigetz!"* (What shall I say to the big fellow?) I suggested he should discuss with him Israel's entry into the Common Market. But Eshkol played ignorant and he asked: "What would we do in the Common Market? Are you sure that we should join? Why?"

I made some remark or other and mentioned the problem of citrus fruit. Eshkol's eyes lit up. "Oranges!" he cried. "A marvelous subject!"

We arrived in Pompidou's ornate office. Everything seemed very correct and well organized. Pompidou even provided his own interpreter, a French rabbi. He invited us to sit, and I sensed that Eshkol was in an irreverent mood.

He began by saying: "My father was born in the Ukraine." Pompidou asked whereabouts in the Ukraine and as he did so his face began to show signs of doubt: what did Eshkol's father have to do with this official meeting? This expression of doubt intensified as Eshkol went on with his lecture: his

* The Hotel Matignon is the Prime Minister's residence.

father owned a flour mill, to which the peasants brought their grain; in this mill he had acquired a taste for agriculture; he brought this taste with him to Palestine; he had been a farmer in Degania; in Degania there was malaria; the heat was unbearable; the soil was uncooperative; and yet in spite of all this they had grown bananas and tried to grow grapefruit; the members of the kibbutz had competed among themselves to see who could dig the most irrigation ditches around the trees. . . .

And when Eshkol came round to citrus fruits, to oranges, his eyes lit up and his excitement grew and grew. He went on to tell Pompidou how we had increased our fruit-growing capacity fourfold over the last fifteen years; how we had improved the strains, enriched the soil, and devised means of saving water. It was as if he was unable to get away from the subject of agriculture. At last he came round to the Common Market and explained to the French Prime Minister that a high tariff wall was liable to endanger the fruits of pioneering enterprises. Therefore France and Israel should also cooperate in the spheres of agriculture and science.

As this impassioned address proceeded, Pompidou became more and more embarrassed. He could not understand how these things were connected and where they were leading. When Eshkol finished speaking, Pompidou said a few words in praise of the Common Market, and then he took a deep breath and launched into a fascinating discourse on "The place of the apple in Greek mythology"; Pompidou had at one time been a lecturer in mythology. Three goddesses—Artemis, goddess of nature and hunting; Athene, goddess of wisdom; and Aphrodite, goddess of beauty and love—asked Paris, the son of the king of Troy, to decide which of them was the most beautiful and to award an apple to the winner; he chose Aphrodite. Or Heracles, for example, Pompidou continued, who was ordered to bring back golden apples from the Garden of the Hesperides; Heracles was compelled to undertake this impossible mission and he succeeded in it. Since then the apple, together with Heracles, has become symbolic of the attainment of the impossible. . . . As Pompidou warmed to his subject, Eshkol looked more and more astonished. Now it was his turn to wonder where the conversation was leading. Pompidou ended his lecture with the comment: 'I once taught others about the source of the golden apples. Now I have been taught where they come from.'*

As we left, Eshkol was both baffled and amused and he asked me in Yiddish: *"Was hat der Goy gewalt?"* (What did the goy want?)

The liveried attendants opened the gates, and a new "problem" presented itself. Outside the palace there were hordes of French and Israeli journalists, television cameramen and radio reporters. "Oh dear," said Eshkol, "what are we going to tell them?" I said: "Perhaps you should say that we have been discussing the Common Market and scientific

---

* TRANSLATOR'S NOTE: the Hebrew word for "orange" literally means "golden apple."

and agricultural cooperation." Eshkol thought for a moment and said: "In that case, you can do the talking."

I broke into a cold sweat. But I had no choice. I made a brief statement and refused to comment further. The next day the newspaper headlines reported negotiations on "Scientific and agricultural cooperation" and mentioned the fact that "government spokesmen" had refused to go into detail. From a political point of view this meeting was of little significance, but as a human experience it had been a most enjoyable example of the juicy Eshkolian approach.

I observed quite a different Eshkol—aggressive, serious and sensitive—during his visit to President Johnson, and again in 1964. We left on a Sunday morning and arrived in the United States after an eighteen-hour flight. It had been decided that we should land initially in Philadelphia, rather than Washington, and this both for symbolic reasons (Philadelphia having been the first capital of America) and for the sake of our comfort (allowing us to overcome the effects of jet lag and thus to arrive in Washington more relaxed). At the site of the Liberty Bell there was a welcome ceremony in honor of the Israeli Prime Minister. Jewish children waved blue and white flags and sang the national anthem of Israel. Eshkol's eyes filled with tears (all the members of his entourage were similarly affected), and afterwards we visited the Philadelphia City Museum to see an exhibition of sculptures by Lipschitz.

Eshkol was being accompanied on this trip by

Yaakov Herzog, Teddy Kollek, and myself. We were also joined by our ambassador Abe Harman, who brought with him the draft of a joint communiqué to be published at the end of our visit to the United States. Such visits usually begin at the end—with an agreed draft of the final communiqué.

We began our consultations at 10 P.M. Most of us were already exhausted, but Eshkol was as fresh as if he had just woken up. He read the draft communiqué and got furious: it contained no guarantee to assist the security of Israel. This was a point of great importance. At that time we were extremely anxious at the rumors (rumors which soon turned out to be well founded) that the United States intended to supply tanks to Jordan. Our request had been turned down. The Americans were also refusing to supply the planes that we had asked for.

Also on the agenda for discussion was the subject of the construction in Israel of an atomic reactor for desalination purposes. The Americans insisted on their right to supervise any nuclear project in Israel. We needed firm assurances that supervision of the reactor would not become supervision of the State as a whole.

On the way to the United States, Eshkol told me that he intended to take a hard line on all these points. And he was as good as his word. He told Harman that if this was to be the communiqué, it would be better that there be no communiqué at all, and he was prepared to call off the entire visit there and then.

Abe telephoned the State Department and passed on the information that the Prime Minister was determined not to agree to the joint communiqué, unless a clause was added guaranteeing the defense needs of the State of Israel. These negotiations by telephone lasted, with occasional breaks for consultation, until the early hours of the morning, when the State Department promised to submit to the President a draft corresponding to our demands.

Next morning we flew to Washington in the presidential helicopter. Eshkol was uneasy. He told me in a whisper that if his demands were not met —there would be no joint communiqué.

On the lawn of the White House there was an impressive official reception ceremony. (Everybody's name was printed on a card, and these cards were laid out on the lawn, so that we should know where to stand.) The crowd behind the fence clapped enthusiastically. Eshkol turned to me again and said: "Idiots! Why are they clapping, we haven't achieved anything yet!"

We were shown into the Oval Room. Johnson sat down in the rocking chair which had belonged to Kennedy, his predecessor, and we took our places on the sofa beside him. Johnson, who was a man of exceptional stature, almost a giant, seemed quite relaxed. First of all, he shot an inquisitive glance at Eshkol. Then he picked up a sheet of paper from the desk in front of him, and read aloud: *"The USA stands four square behind Israel."*

Eshkol glanced at me mischievously, as if to

say: you see, bonus! After this initial promise came the list of items around which the previous night's discussions had centered. Eshkol breathed a sigh of relief. It was all there—the question of arms, the desalination plant and methods of supervision. Eshkol replied with gratitude and with a lecture on the situation of Israel. And once again he began with an account of the history of Degania. But unlike Pompidou, Johnson was clearly interested in what Eshkol had to say: he was a farmer himself. Agriculture and the pioneering spirit and living by the Scriptures were things very close to his heart—a Texan heart with a deep awareness of the pioneering history of America. An instinctive rapport was forged between them, and Eshkol, encouraged by Johnson's reaction, went further with his story, which began to sound more and more like a legend from another world. He was speaking as if to a like-minded person, with sincerity and persuasiveness, talking about settlement, immigration and defense.

When we had taken our leave of the President he exclaimed: *"Junger mann*—four square! That's what he said. Four square, not three. And he's put that clause in the agreement. But you can't fight with clauses. We shall have to talk to him about tanks." It was, therefore, agreed that I should meet the President's adviser, Averell Harriman, to work out the details of the "final draft." In the meantime we heard the news that an American ship was already unloading Patton tanks in the port of Aqaba. We felt somewhat cheated and gravely concerned.

Harriman invited me to lunch in his office. He opened a bottle of vodka and said: "Let's drink to the taste, not to the maker. . . . I know them both, and there's quite a difference." Then he said more seriously: "I know that you want to see Johnson elected for a second term. And you know that we want Eshkol to continue in office. Let's see how we can help each other."

I told Harriman that nobody could remain in office as Prime Minister of Israel without proving to his people, in practical terms, his ability to guarantee their defense needs.

"The trauma of the War of Independence still haunts us. You, the Americans, voted for us in the United Nations. But when the Arab States attacked us, you even refused to give us rifles. Eshkol cannot go home empty-handed. Especially now that an American ship is delivering tanks to Jordan."

Harriman knew about the secret negotiations that we were holding with the Germans for the supply of tanks to Israel. He wanted to know exactly what the situation was, and said that at this stage it would be better to help us through Germany, rather than directly.

I returned to Eshkol and told him the gist of the conversation. "If that's the way it is," he said, "we shall have to bring it up with Johnson again." In the meeting that afternoon he spoke bluntly, and straight to the point. He put down on the table his demand for supplies of tanks and planes. President Johnson repeated what his adviser had said but added that if nothing came of the deal with Germany, the United States would supply us with the necessary arms direct. As for planes, he would send a mission to Israel to discuss it with us.

Eshkol was not satisfied with this answer. He wanted to know how it would be decided, and by whom, whether the German deal had succeeded or failed.

Then Johnson mentioned that the German Chancellor, Erhard, was due to visit the United States the following week, and he suggested that I should stay in Washington for another week, during which time it should become clear how the deal would work out. Eshkol accepted this suggestion. And so I did indeed stay on for a week as the guest of the American Government in the guise of a distinguished visitor from Nepal. The hotel management promoted me accordingly, and as a mark of respect to the Prime Minister of Nepal, they hoisted the Nepalese flag from the mast.

Eventually the tanks left Germany, loaded on transports. On the way to Rome they had to pass through an ancient gate, and the turret of one of the tanks became caught in the arch. Efforts were made to extricate the tank without damaging the gate. In the meantime local traffic was held up for several hours, and the cause of the delay became known to the press. With the veil of secrecy torn, Germany was forced to withdraw from the deal and as a result we received tanks from the United States. Later a deputation from the United States—Averell Harriman and Bob Comer, Deputy Adviser to the President on National Security—arrived in Israel. After lengthy round-the-clock negotiations we finally arrived at an agreement promising us supplies of American aircraft.

Eshkol conducted the negotiations for receiving a desalination plant. Following the negotiations with the Committee for Atomic Energy, Israel signed an agreement which limited supervision only to the experimental reactor at Nebi-Rubin.

Eshkol, "the compromiser," was not prepared to compromise on this occasion, and the results of our American visit vindicated his firm stand.

President Johnson held a state banquet in our honor. After the meal and the music, there was dancing. Johnson invited Mrs. Miriam Eshkol to join him in the first waltz. Abe Harman approached Eshkol and said: "Levi, you ought to invite Lady Bird to dance with you." Eshkol winked at Harman and replied in Yiddish: *"Mein toyer Ambassador, ich tanse nicht!"* (My dear Ambassador, I don't dance!) Then he turned to me and said: *"Junger mann,* this is a job for you. You're always saying that we should give the younger generation a chance!" The laughter at this remark relieved us all from the tension that we were still feeling. Another visit took place in 1964.

I presented Eshkol with a plan and an estimate of the cost. He glanced briefly at the paper that I showed him and frowned. "Fifty million! That's a colossal sum. Have you ever counted up to a million? And fifty million is fifty times that. Anyway, why is it so much?" And then I suggested that we go and see a similar program in operation, so that he could form an impression of the plant and equipment on the spot. The idea appealed to him. Although he was as sparing of pennies as he was of millions, Eshkol was fascinated by large projects. And since I knew this, I was not discouraged by his initial refusal.

We contacted friends in Italy and it was agreed that we should travel by Israeli Air Force plane to an airbase in Naples, and fly from there to Sardinia. I asked our military attaché in Italy, Reuven Cari, to find us a place to stay overnight, so that we could avoid using a hotel and thus attracting attention. Not far from Naples, Cari found a deserted palace that had once served as a lodge for visiting Bourbon kings.

From outside the palace looked magnificent, inside—nothing worked. The doors did not close, the water in the taps was full of rust, and the furniture was decrepit. This was in winter, and the palace was icy cold. Eshkol uttered not a word of complaint, on the contrary, he was in a jovial mood: "So this is your idea of economy!" And when Eshkol put aside his Prime Minister's cloak for a day or two it was as if he forgot his age as well, and he turned into a mischievous child.

We hired a carriage, and Ezer Weizmann (then the commander of the Air Force) sat beside the driver and took the reins and the whip. We began riding up and down the narrow winding streets of Naples. Eshkol seemed in high spirits. In the afternoon our Italian hosts invited us to tour Capri. To the astonishment of the Italians, Eshkol insisted on climbing into the cable car and riding up to the top of the mountain. We were all infected with his *joie de vivre* and all those present, Italians as well as Israelis, suddenly found themselves behaving like naughty children.

The following day we flew to Sardinia. From far away we saw the red roofs of the villas built on the seashore by the Aga Khan. We landed at an airfield close to the testing site which was a mass of antennae, weird contraptions and tall white buildings with tops like church spires. Inside these buildings were computers and white-coated laboratory technicians.

Just as humor was Eshkol's flower, practical activity was his finest fruit. Here he showed himself inquisitive and thirsty for practical actions. The calculations which he had heard and investigated and assessed sounded hollow, almost derisory, when he repeated them, but his true inclination was quite different: to act, to act boldly and decisively. On this occasion he did not call me *"Junger mann"* but "Reb* Shimon."

"How long would it take us to build one of these, Mr. Shimon? It would cost double the esti-

---

* "Reb" is a Yiddish affectionate diminutive for "Mr."

mate, I think. And it would never be complete and fully operational, is that not true?" But in spite of this noncommittal statement it was easy to tell that he was eager for action and that he expected me to supply answers that would make the decision easier and more tempting, justifying the conclusion that he had already reached in his heart.

Eshkol avoided abstract discussion. There was a purpose to all the questions that he asked and he needed to see with his own eyes before he was convinced. In the matter of the atomic plant in Dimona he made it clear to me that he did not want any detail, any conceivable doubt kept from him.

"Aren't you wasting good money?" he would say. "Experts don't tell you the truth and you can't find it out for yourself." But when proposals were put forward that the project be canceled—he stood by us. And so it was on this occasion too.

In fact, when he boarded the plane for Sardinia his mind was already made up. The purpose of the visit was confirmation, not decision. And at the end of our trip he said: "The money we don't have. But we must find it." And on the way home I already knew that not only were the two of us in partnership, I would also be under constant pressure from him. He would call me on the telephone at impossible times and ask: "What's the situation? Have you built anything yet?"

This was the constructive Eshkol. The Eshkol who founded the Mekorot ("Water resources") company and founded it in a very "Eshkolian" way. On the eve of the Second World War he traveled to Germany for the purpose of transferring Jewish property to Israel. "You can't shift houses," he told me later, "pipes you can shift. If you have pipes, you can irrigate. If you can irrigate, you have fountains." With characteristic humor he added: "When I was secretary of the Tel Aviv Labor Council, I went one day to Brenner House. In one of the rooms I saw a large nail on the wall. I said to myself: there's a nail, a picture should be hung on it. And now, instead of an empty wall with a protruding nail, there's a wall with a fine picture on it."

Eshkol acted in similar vein when he began establishing settlements in the Negev. When his colleagues in the Party Central Committee asked him how the settlers would make a living, he replied: "Grass, they will grow grass and eat grass."

Eshkol had one outstanding quality: he would tell a man uncomplimentary things *to his face.* He would say the complimentary things behind his back.

At the time of the outbreak of the War of Independence, a certain woman asked if he would see her. "What is it about?" he asked, and she replied, "A personal matter." With clear reluctance he agreed to talk to her. "Look," he said to me, "she will come, make some request that I will never be able to grant, and she will bear me a grudge for the rest of her life."

His prediction was nearly accurate. The woman arrived. Her face was grim and she had great difficulty in speaking. She was a widow, and her only son had been conscripted and sent to the front. Since then she had been unable to sleep, she felt that this was an ordeal that she could not endure. Eshkol tried to explain to her that it was not in his power to help. First, it was difficult to send instructions to front-line troops; second, this was not his responsibility and the army did not want this kind of interference; third, according to the regulations there was no need for the boy to be sent to the front unless he had volunteered for it of his own free will, as he had apparently done in this case, against his mother's wishes; fourth, he, Eshkol, could not and would not make a promise that he would be unable to keep.

The woman left him deeply disappointed, her eyes full of tears. But the moment that she was out of the room, Eshkol began "moving heaven and earth." He rang the head of the Personnel Branch, the Deputy Chief of Staff and the Divisional Commander and he did not rest until he had discovered the soldier's whereabouts. And the following day he continued with his efforts until the young man had been transferred to an auxiliary unit.

I am sure that the mother does not know to this day what went on between her leaving Eshkol's office and the moment that her son was moved to a safer place.

In every argument he made an effort to see both sides of the coin; it was as a result of this that he was seen as a compromiser, or as a man seized by indecision.

Another episode, of central importance and extremely distressing, tested his qualities to the full and led ultimately to a deep and painful schism: the "Lavon Affair."

At this point I should make it clear that I was fond of Eshkol and that I admired him. He had a decisive effect on the course of my life. It was Eshkol who came to Kibbutz Alumot in June 1947 with a letter from David Ben-Gurion instructing me to join the Staff of the Haganah. Even before then he had helped me in my Working Youth activities. He entrusted me with a great many duties and every now and then, in times of crisis, he would draw me out in conversation, advising me to consult David Ben-Gurion on personal and professional matters. When he was elected Prime Minister and Minister of Defense, he approached me again and asked me to continue serving as Deputy Minister of Defense, the post which I had held in Ben-Gurion's administration, and naturally I was glad to be working with him again.

It never occurred to me that one day I would be thrown into a position of unprecedented difficulty, and that the episode would end with a total break between us, against my will and contrary to all my expectations and hopes.

Eshkol found it impossible to understand Ben-Gurion's viewpoint in the "Lavon Affair." He would ask again and again: "Why is Ben-Gurion taking this business so seriously? What is he really fighting for? A principle? A tactical advantage? And why does

Ben-Gurion believe the word of a senior officer rather than that of Pinhas Lavon? After all, it was Ben-Gurion who appointed Lavon Minister of Defense, against the advice of his colleagues."

One day, at the beginning of the "Affair," I was in Eshkol's car, traveling with him from Jerusalem to Tel Aviv.

"What does Ben-Gurion want in the Lavon business?" he asked me.

I replied that I did not believe that Ben-Gurion *wanted* anything in the Lavon business. He was fighting for a principle, for the truth. Ben-Gurion feared that in our society, even in its highest echelons, there was a tendency to obscure the truth, and that this tendency would bring disaster on our people. If members of the Government were to compromise over the truth, over the fearless and unequivocal pursuit of the truth, then they were liable to recoil from the truth in circumstances where the fate of the nation was hanging in the balance.

"Are you sure," he asked, probing me further, "that the truth is all that he is concerned with?"

"Yes," I replied simply.

"I see, and do you believe that it is possible to discover the truth and the whole truth?"

"We must try."

"And if you know the truth, do you always tell it? To everyone? To your wife? Your friends? Do you tell other people *everything* that you have done?"

Eshkol tried to appease Ben-Gurion but at the same time found himself at odds with him. He remained skeptical and refused to be convinced that this was a fight for the highest motives. He suspected that there was some unintelligible elements in all this, some Machiavellian ploy. The relations between him and Ben-Gurion became more and more acrimonious. Ben-Gurion did not like compromise on matters of principle, while Eshkol was not prepared to cooperate in something that looked to him like surrender to Ben-Gurion's caprice.

The criticism leveled at the Prime Minister following the visit to Britain by the minister Yosef Almogi, prompted Eshkol to say that if one or two members of the Government disagreed with his methods, they must draw their own conclusions. Almogi decided to resign, and being his ally as a supporter of Ben-Gurion, I decided to resign as well as a gesture of solidarity. I told Eshkol of my intention to resign, and he invited me to talk it over with him, in the hope of persuading me to stay on. David Ben-Gurion also sent me a message from Sdeh Boker, urging me not to give up my post since "defense takes precedence over everything." But I kept to my decision: I had come to the conclusion that it was impossible to go on working with Eshkol, and at the same time to support Ben-Gurion, who was beginning to oppose him actively.

We parted on friendly terms, and at a farewell party held in the Prime Minister's garden, Eshkol paid me some generous compliments.

I was elected secretary of the Rafi movement that we launched in June 1965. We were obliged to organize ourselves very quickly in order to compete in the elections scheduled for November of the same year. These were months of backbreaking work. We started out with nothing—no money, no office, no provincial branches. The people who rallied around Rafi were a distinguished group, including Moshe Dayan, Nathan Alterman, S. Yizhar, Yitzhak Navon, Professor E. D. Bergmann, Teddy Kollek, Yosef Almogi, Gad Yaakobi, Matilda Ghuez, and others. We had a common background and close personal links, but we were not accustomed to working together in the context of a political party. And our leader was David Ben-Gurion, whose movements were unpredictable: it was difficult to guess what he would say, where and with how much intensity.

We stood beside Ben-Gurion and naturally we backed up his pronouncements. He began with a ferocious attack on Eshkol, declaring that Eshkol had characteristics unsuited to the office of Prime Minister, and that he lacked the characteristics essential for a Prime Minister. . . . The quarrel intensified. The friendly relations of many years changed into a deep and uncompromising hostility.

After the 1965 elections I made the principal opposition speech on behalf of Rafi, the first time that I had ever spoken against Levi Eshkol. Eshkol replied with a mixture of annoyance and pleasure: "You're worse than Begin. But your Hebrew is all right."

For two years, between the 1965 elections and the Six Day War, we met on few occasions. On the eve of the war, on account of the indecision which Eshkol's Government was showing, my colleagues and I, with David Ben-Gurion at our head, became convinced that the time had come to act decisively and establish a government of national unity, a government that would take preemptive action against the danger, that appeared strong, threatening and immediate. We contacted many members of Mapai, of Gahal and Mafdal. Menachem Begin asked me if Ben-Gurion was "ready and able to be Prime Minister." I replied: "Able—yes; ready—I don't know."

I mentioned this conversation to Ben-Gurion, with whom I was in constant touch, almost day and night. Ben-Gurion did not confide in me as to whether he was prepared to serve as Prime Minister again, but he vehemently demanded the replacement of Eshkol.

Through contacts with the various parties, it became clear to me that there was not a majority in favor of Eshkol's removal, and all that could be achieved immediately was the appointment of Moshe Dayan as Minister of Defense. But in the meantime Eshkol summoned Dayan and offered him command of the Southern Front, which Moshe was willing to accept. And he sent Avraham Ofer to me, inviting me to join the coalition Government as Minister Without Portfolio. I declined, of course, even though Moshe Dayan called me on the telephone that day and said: "Shimon, all your efforts are in vain, you won't achieve anything." I stood firm and insisted that Dayan join the government as

Minister of Defense, as I saw this as an essential precondition for the establishment of a Government of national unity which would decide on the commencement of war, and bring success in the battle itself.

Then came one of the most difficult moments of my life: I was obliged to go to Ben-Gurion and tell him that there was no prospect of removing Eshkol, and that we must be content with the appointment of Moshe Dayan to the Ministry of Defense. I knew in advance that Ben-Gurion's reaction would be furious.

I visited him on the Thursday morning, accompanied by a colleague, and described the entire situation in detail.

He erupted like a volcano.

"I thought," he thundered at me, "that you were a statesman and a friend. Now I'm in doubt on both scores. Don't you understand that Eshkol is incapable of being a war leader? Did we not agree that the condition for our participation in the Government was to be the replacement of the Prime Minister?"

I knew that there was no alternative in this argument but to answer him back with equal ferocity and ruthlessness:

"Ben-Gurion, you are fond of saying that if the whole weight of ideological consideration is placed on one side of the scales, and the requirements of defense on the other, the defense side must outweigh the other. Does this rule only govern us, or does it apply to you too? Don't you see what our defense position is? And you know exactly how much our influence in the Knesset is worth."

The volcano subsided as suddenly as it had erupted. Ben-Gurion embraced me and said: "I'm sorry, I have wronged you."

The conversation became calmer, and Ben-Gurion asked me to describe the balance of forces and the latest news from the front. After a while I noticed that a glint had suddenly appeared in his eye, and I realized that I was in for a surprise.

"I understand your thinking and I trust your logic and your sincerity. But my opinion of Eshkol has not changed. I agree that we should join the Government, on condition that you go to Eshkol and tell him that even after we have joined the Government, we shall have no confidence in his leadership."

I shuddered, but I knew that without this bitter pill, confusion and dissension would continue at a time when our soldiers were already preparing to engage the enemy.

I was depressed the whole of that day. In the evening there was a small dinner-party at Ben-Gurion's house. Everybody present gave me their enthusiastic support, and Ben-Gurion was the most generous of all. But their compliments did not make my life any easier; the worst was still before me.

Eshkol's secretary called me and asked me to pass on our decision. We arranged a meeting for the following day, Friday morning. I asked Yitzhak Navon to accompany me. Eshkol greeted us warmly, as if nothing had happened between us. He offered us tea, putting a lavish portion of sliced lemon in his own cup, as had always been his habit. We told him Rafi's decision (which of course he already knew), and Eshkol said he was sure that this decision was the right one. He also welcomed my assurance that "Rafi is prepared to reunite with Mapai without preconditions." At the end of the meeting I asked to be left alone with Eshkol for a *tête-a-tête* conversation.

I began by saying: "I greatly regret that it is my duty to inform you of another message, not an easy or a pleasant one, but it has one merit—it is the naked truth at this time. As you know," I continued, "our belief is that you are not fitted to be Prime Minister, and this view of ours still applies. Of course, once we have joined the Government, we shall cooperate with total loyalty, and all personal opinions and prejudices will be set aside."

As I spoke these words I was blushing and sweating profusely. There was no way of avoiding this painful mission, but at the same time I felt that I was putting enormous pressure on a man who, in spite of all that had happened recently, was still very dear to me.

I believe that Eshkol sensed what I was going through. His reply was calm, even forgiving: "I understand that this is your position, perhaps you will revise it again sometime."

On leaving his room I breathed a sigh of relief. I wondered where I should go next. The natural destination was David Ben-Gurion's house. The old lion was at his home in Keren Kayemet Boulevard, Tel Aviv, lonely and tormented, angry, afraid and as perceptive as ever. I arrived in Keren Kayemet Boulevard, but instead of going to Ben-Gurion's house I went into a small café nearby and called Eshkol's office once again. I asked him for another meeting, as a matter of urgency. A few hours later we met. He looked pleased but puzzled as well: what did I have to say now?

I began by saying: "This time I am here unofficially, not on behalf of the Movement nor of the Party. Tomorrow or the day after the guns will start to roar. This is war, and nobody knows how it will end and what the future holds for the people and the State. Is it really necessary for us to go into this war with dissension at the highest level? I believe that the time has come for a reconciliation between David Ben-Gurion and yourself. All that has happened in the past is insignificant compared with what awaits us tomorrow and the day after."

Eshkol stopped me for a moment, puzzled and greatly astonished, and asked: "What do you suggest that I do?"

"Don't ask anyone's advice, get in your car and drive to Keren Kayemet Boulevard, go to Ben-Gurion's house and tell him that we are on the brink of war and that the past should be forgotten." And I added: "If I may, I would suggest that you ask Ben-Gurion to leave immediately for the United States and perhaps France as well, to explain to Johnson and De Gaulle and the Jews of the Diaspora, what our situation is and what our only possible course of action is."

Eshkol listened patiently, but he was not convinced: "Supposing I go to Ben-Gurion's house and he refuses to see me? What has happened is quite enough."

I replied: "If you're prepared to give it a try, I'll go and see 'The Old Man' first. I'll tell him that you want to meet him face to face, and if Ben-Gurion raises any doubts, we'll abandon the attempt to straighten things out between you, which is so essential at this time."

Eshkol's view of Ben-Gurion was most ambivalent: his admiration for Ben-Gurion never wavered, but it was combined with a deep sense of injury and pain, a feeling that the old man had turned against him for no reason, and treated him quite unfairly.

Eshkol thought for a while and then said: "There is something in your suggestion. Let me think it over and I'll let you know later today."

I left his office in rather better spirits. The prospect of a reconciliation between Ben-Gurion and Eshkol was so important to me that I hoped that with this gesture the circle would be closed, and the grudges of the past forgotten.

Disappointment came quickly. In the evening Eshkol called me from Jerusalem and said: "Shimon, I have given a lot of thought to your suggestion. I understand your motives. But I can't accept it just now. Some other time perhaps."

This episode haunted me for a long time. More

than ten years have passed since then, and a great many things have changed. Old wounds have begun to heal and yet I still painfully regret the fact that the two men, who had once been such close friends, were never to be reconciled, and that they both died while still in a state of deep and bitter feud.

Eshkol was a man of action and a romantic. He loved playing with numbers. He would break down every suggestion to its tiniest components, like a watchmaker who dismantles the minutest wheels, to discover the secret of the moving hands.

But this was only his outward appearance. The basis of his personality was his love of building and creation. He built, and he was in love with what he built. He loved the ground, water, workshops. He loved the courage of creation and the boldness of men of action. In fact, he had no inclination for details: he preferred the artist's brush to the architect's ruler.

One day he visited a Mekorot project, at the Gilboa Station. The pumping machinery was bathed in a sea of green—grass, trees and flowers. Eshkol was deeply impressed and intoxicated at the sight. He acted true to form, however, and turning to me he said: "Do you remember Pushkin? And how he wrote in one of his poems 'I have to build myself a monument—not of stone. And the people's path to it shall not sprout grass.' Well, I tell you—I planted this grass, but it's the grass of our people, not of one man."

Eshkol was a fine looking man and one to catch

the eyes of women. But he himself did not take his masculine appeal seriously.

"They say girls, like industrial enterprises, are drawn to me. But it's not true, I'm the one who is drawn to them. . . ."

He was drawn and he also drew. He knew how to animate people, infecting them with his enthusiasm and faith.

I remember the time that Eshkol came to Kibbutz Geva to recruit me into the Youth Movement secretariat. He arrived at the kibbutz full of boyish vitality and charm. And when his mission had been accomplished, he invited me to go back with him to his home in Degania. When we arrived at the main road, we saw a large stone on the right hand side. Eshkol glanced at the road, at the traffic, and at the stone. "It is possible," he said, thinking aloud, "to pass the stone on the left, which is what logic demands, and it is possible to pass it on the right, which is what the traffic laws demand; we certainly cannot go over it. And there is another possibility." He stopped the car and announced solemnly: "We are going to get out and move the stone! Why? First, the road will be cleared. Drivers who follow us will not be faced with a problem. And second, we will not only be doing our duty to logic and the law, we shall also have achieved something."

Then suddenly: "Why travel on the main road, when there are unpaved tracks?" He turned the car eastward and after a few minutes we were near Ein Harod. "I ask you," he said, "what are they doing with such an elegant water fountain? I wonder if it could be sent to the South? These fields are fertile —even meager farmers could be settled here." And glancing at the Gilboa he added: "Even Jews could be talked into living up there. We already have some 'climbers' in the Planning Division—let's give them a mountain and they'll plant vines and fruit-trees and then they'll really see life."

Eshkol's landscape was basic and primordial: the sea and the land, the valley and the hill, and the creative experience of man turning a naked dream-picture into a concrete reality, in which people walk about, flourish and continue to dream. Eshkol was drawn to such landscapes and he harnessed them to his artistic talent, which was both lyrical and pro-saic.

His Zionism was agricultural Zionism. Furrows in the soil meant as much to him as did the charms of philosophy and his personality was as purposeful as the purpose of life itself. His faith was steadfast —without moods and changes. His faith, his sobri-ety and his optimism, combined with a unique sense of humor, enabled him to draw together people of differing temperaments and conflicting energies and direct them toward creative activity. A great thinker, he was also a high flier, a central figure among the most daring and illustrious visionaries of his people.

In defense matters he was an activist. As a member of the Haganah Command, as Deputy Min-ister of Defense, as Treasurer, as Minister of Defense

—he contributed greatly to the strengthening of our defense capacity. He knew that in questions of defense it is vital to first recognize the danger and only then to consider the price; to look to the demands of tomorrow, not to the achievements of yesterday. He was not worried by the strength of our enemies, but he feared our own weakness. As a Jew he knew that our true strength lies within us, in our inner selves, in the modest but positive faith that confounds all expectations, and makes what is impossible today the certain promise of tomorrow, with the dawning of the day on the true landscape.

BERL KATZNELSON
A Tearing Intellect

His love for all Israel did not impair his love for individuals in Israel.

S. Y. AGNON ON BERL

ANYONE WHO HAD the privilege of meeting Berl in his lifetime gained an unforgettable experience. Even today, thirty years after his death, meeting him has not lost its flavor. To this very day, more than fifty years after his appearance in the Labor movement of Eretz Israel, his inspiration is still with us. Both that which he created and that which he prevented have strongly influenced the character and the conduct of the Jewish Labor movement and of the State of Israel as a whole.

Berl was the cornerstone of the Labor movement; he showed the way and he was the fountain from which flowed the original and constructive spirit of the Labor movement in our country. It is possible that without him, and without the colleagues for whom he was, in Ben-Gurion's words, "the leader of the pack," Israel would have been deprived of its uniqueness and cut off from its roots in and its link with the Judean state of the Second Temple period; the two would have been similar only inasmuch as modern Greece is similar to ancient Greece. He gave us a philosophical rationale for our national existence here, and his contribution to the shaping of this philosophy was both diverse and original. He cherished ideas, trained people and founded enterprises such as *Davar*, the workers' newspaper; Am Oved, the publishing house of the Histadrut; organizations giving aid to individuals and projects, and more.

Berl died in 1944, at the age of fifty-seven. The writings that he left behind have since been collected in thirteen volumes; they contain some of the finest Hebrew prose ever written and some of the most profound thinking ever expressed in the language. He left behind him a generation of poets, writers, scholars, men of action and soldiers, the future leaders of the State of Israel.

I saw him for the last time three days before his death, in Rotenberg House on Mount Carmel, where he was conducting a seminar for youth leaders. He was deeply attached to this house, as he was to the man whose name it bears: Pinhas Rotenberg. A spacious house in a charming corner of Mount Carmel, its design reflects Rotenberg's love of things with large dimensions: lofty rooms and balconies over-looking the beautiful landscape of Carmel.

That evening Berl was again suffering from severe headaches and he looked tired and anxious. He way lying on a small settee in a room set aside for his use. This was at a time of serious dissension within the General Council of Hanoar Haoved (Young Labor), and as I was a member of the Secretariat, Berl wanted to hear from me about all the latest developments. He asked questions, listened and replied this way or that. I remember how he pointed to the massive wall and said grimly: "You see this strong wall? Although it understands nothing, it too will disintegrate, it too will split. Disintegration has a logic of its own."

On the Sunday morning I heard that Berl had died on Saturday evening. I was then a member of Kibbutz Alumot. Using the motor bike loaned to me by the movement, I immediately set out for Afula to join his funeral cortège on its way from Jerusalem to Kinneret. On the outskirts of Afula the road was already jammed by the crowds coming to pay him their last respects. They came on foot, in cars, in carts, in tractors. There were Yemenites with curling earlocks and girls in working clothes. There were kibbutz veterans, their open-necked shirts revealing tanned chests covered in graying hair. There were long-haired poets too, and pillars of the Establishment. It was as if the whole population of Eretz Israel, young and old, was moving northward, to take leave of Berl on his last journey.

I felt a strong sense of loneliness and bereavement and I knew that many people in the crowd felt the same, as if we had all suffered not only a collective loss, but a personal one too. In my imagination I went back six years, to my first meeting with Berl.

I was then studying at the Ben-Shemen youth village, to which Mulla Cohen and I had been sent by the Tel Aviv branch of Hanoar Haoved to instill a basic knowledge of the land in the young immigrants who lived in the village.

We were both experiencing for the first time the taste of independent living, in a village populated entirely by young people. We lost no opportunity to enjoy our independence and even to draw attention to it by absenting ourselves from classes. Sometimes we disobeyed our supervisors and teachers and went out by ourselves to stroll in the rocky Judean hills, which in spring were covered with wild flowers, cyclamen and anemones. We climbed trees and gorged ourselves with sweet-tasting green and brown figs. We loved literature and poetry; Zalman Shneour's *The Pearl Fishers* appealed to our thirst for adventure and Heinrich Heine's *Paris Diaries* to our sense of cynicism. When I met Sonya—my future wife— for the first time, I read her extracts from Karl Marx's *Kapital,* and I was convinced that this would have the desired effect. Sonya lived in her parents' house which was next to a Haganah position. I used to do sentry duty there at night, after we had sworn an oath of loyalty to the Haganah on the Bible and a revolver, by candlelight.

The youth village of Ben-Shemen, which was

surrounded by vegetation, lawns, flowers and trees, was established to train young people—most of them immigrants, with a minority of native Israelis —for the life of agriculture and comradeship. Its graduates set up farms and collective settlements. During this period it was surrounded on all sides by Arab villages and at night—these were the troubled years of 1936–39—the village was a target for gangs of Arab snipers. We used to arrive at the village in armored cars, since we had to pass through Lod and Ramle where the inhabitants pelted us with stones and sometimes even with Molotov cocktails.

The village looked like the green base of a dark brown basin. Inside, pastoral tranquillity reigned; outside, the Arab threat steadily mounted.

The village teachers, under the leadership of Dr. Lehman, tried hard to cultivate in us an interest in music, in painting, in literature and in agricultural work. At the same time they forbade political activity, or the setting up of a branch of Hanoar Haoved among the younger age groups, who were organized into what was known in village parlance as "The Children's Association," as opposed to "The Youth Association" to which we belonged.

It is hardly surprising that we should have decided, in defiance of the village authorities, to establish a secret branch of our organization. And because of its clandestine nature, the best of the children were drawn to it. Our meetingplace was the mule shed.

At the time, I described the atmosphere of the

village and its surroundings in some articles published in *Bama'aleh,* the weekly newspaper of Hanoar Haoved. I never imagined that this paper was also read by Berl. I was very surprised when one morning I received a message from Berl, telling me that he had read my articles, had enjoyed them, and was inviting me to meet him at his home in Mazeh Street, Tel Aviv.

I arrived at the appointed time, one Sunday evening, and I climbed the stairs in some haste. The door opened, and I found myself in a room full of books, pamphlets and newspapers, some of them piled up and some scattered about, in various languages: Hebrew, Yiddish, English, German, Russian. There was very little space left for furniture: a table, two or three chairs and a narrow settee, which had a red cover with black stripes.

Previously I had seen Berl in photographs, but his appearance astonished me when I met him face to face. His head was adorned with a mass of black and graying curls. Beneath this tangled mane a firm rectangular forehead protruded, framed by a pair of smooth temples. It was as if the broad forehead shielded the bright intelligent eyes, which moved constantly from side to side. When these eyes were fixed on you in a hard and penetrating stare, it was as if the change in facial expression changed the entire atmosphere in the room.

To my surprise Berl was—like David Ben-Gurion—a man of small stature. His body occupied no more than half the length of the settee; his voice was soft and caressing, and when he held out his hand to me I felt warm and flattered, as if I was a man whom he really wanted to meet, and as if we had known each other for a long time.

Berl questioned me briefly about my surname, Persky, and he asked me if I was related to Daniel Persky, the Hebrew writer who lived in New York: he was pleased when I told him that I was. After that he wanted to know what was going on in Ben-Shemen youth village: the number of pupils, their countries of origin, and who were the youth leaders. Among others I mentioned the name of Yizhar Smilansky, in whom Berl took a great interest. He also wanted to know what we were doing in the village, what the security situation was, and who was the local army commander.

He was never content with one answer to a question. Each answer prompted him to ask another question and in the course of two hours I felt that I had been drained of all the information at my disposal, especially in regard to people and their personalities. But not one single question that he asked was harsh or provocative. In spite of this, I told him more than I intended; I told him things that I would have told nobody else, and at the end of the conversation I felt as if I had been in a confessional.

The final part of our conversation was devoted to literary "inquiry." What were I and my colleagues reading? Had I read *On The Narrow Path* by A. A. Kabak? What did I think of the book, did I find the portrait of Jesus of Nazareth convincing, was the style pleasant to read, and was it in my opinion an important or a mediocre book? He asked if I or my friends had heard of Chaim Hazaz, and he was delighted when I told him that the writings of Hazaz were widely read among our young people. In order to obtain authentic, frank answers, Berl took care not to ask rhetorical questions, such as would give an indication of his own opinions.

We parted after a few hours. I was excited by the experience of meeting the man, by his patience and even more by his unflagging curiosity, also by the very fact that Berl had been prepared to waste a whole evening in the company of a young man, about whom all he had known previously were his name, his place of residence and a few articles published in the youth newspaper.

After this I was invited to his home almost every Sunday. He would direct my attention to important articles published in the newspapers, to books that had been or were about to be published, to poems that he liked; occasionally he would read to me a favorite poem. Whenever he read a poem I felt that he was doing it as much for his own pleasure as for the sake of hospitality. One evening he read to me Bat-Miriam's poems on women of the Bible, on Miriam and Eve and Hagar, and it was clear to me that he was reading these poems with excitement and with pleasure, as if reading them for the first time.

One evening he asked me if I had read the translations of Heinrich Heine which had appeared in

Hebrew, and if I knew who had translated them. I did not know. He told me: "His name is Samuel Perlmann, and he's the son-in-law of a false teeth manufacturer on the Petah Tikvah road." (This factory, Bloom's, was reckoned at the time to be the finest flower of Jewish industry in Palestine.)

"So you see," he added, "how the most unexpected place can produce a talented translator. You should read some of this prose—*The Parliament of Romance, Travel-Sketches, Lucia. . . .*"

I used to sit in his room as if entranced, devouring every word that he spoke, my eyes following every movement of his fine face and every rapid change in his sparkling eyes, which also took part in the conversation, as if in accompaniment.

After he had said his piece, he would begin grilling me. Was I acquainted with Yisrael Galili, who had been one of the founder members of the youth Labor movement? When I said that I was, and expressed admiration for Galili's wisdom and for the Hebrew that he spoke, Berl said: "Yes, that's true. But why did he go and form a new labor organization? Does he not understand the importance of unity within the Labor movement, and the importance of its integrity?" I asked Berl how this had really happened, for it was well known that Galili was Berl's protegé, and that Berl had held great hopes for him, and that Galili revered his master. Berl thought for a moment and then sighed deeply and said: "I may be good at rearing foals, but when the foal becomes a fine horse—I'm a poor driver. . . ."

One evening, when our conversation was nearing its end, Berl asked me what seemed a very strange question: "What do people think and say about David Ben-Gurion?" I told him that the young did not know him at close quarters, and they were exposed to varied and extreme opinions, some paying tribute to his powerful will, his strength of mind, his courage in making decisions and the clarity of his speech, while others were to his disadvantage, alleging him to be vindictive and a bearer of grudges, impatient with the opinions of others, impetuous in debate, and with dictatorial and Bolshevik tendencies.

Berl flared up at this. "Nobody knows Ben-Gurion's shortcomings better than I do. The man is obstinate, he has theatrical tendencies and entrenched opinions and he's like me in that he quarrels with everybody, but he's the greatest Jew that we have, straightforward, strong-minded, and a democrat to his fingertips. He has a great vision in his heart, his spirit is generous and his character firm, without a trace of opportunism or aloofness."

Seldom have I heard such a vehement and spontaneous appraisal of Ben-Gurion. I became aware of the very special kind of friendship existing between the two men, an original, almost romantic friendship. I began to understand that if these two were to join forces they would have the potential to create a whole new movement, a real revolution. Such pairs have worked wonders in history, from Moses and Aaron to Marx and Engels, or Lenin and Trotsky, or

Jaurès and Blum, or Heine and Berne. That evening I learned that all the rumors of a "deep rift" between Ben-Gurion and Berl on account of a "fundamental disagreement" were groundless, and that what we were witnessing was a mighty "pair" in the new history of our people.

My most stimulating encounter with Berl took place on a different occasion. I was informed that the Mahanot Olim (Pioneer Camps) movement, which was purely a student organization, was to hold an ideological seminar in the Ben-Shemen youth village, and that the principal speaker at the seminar was to be Berl Katznelson. I approached Mahanot Olim and asked permission to attend the seminar. Permission was granted, much to my delight.

The youth leaders of Mahanot Olim, the participants in the seminar, were high school graduates, skilled at expressing themselves and noted for their tendency to wrestle with questions of universal importance and to examine things afresh. And there certainly were questions to be wrestled with at that time, in late 1940. The Labor movement and its youth branch were split between two world views: the one tending toward Marxism and Marxist-Leninism in general, the other toward Social Democracy, or "humanistic" Socialism. The advocates of the former viewpoint included the Hashomer Hatzair (Young Guard) movement; this was a young Zionist pioneer organization which had achieved remarkable results in the building of settlements, but whose ideological goal was "the orientation of the world of tomorrow," the central pillars of which were the class war, Marxist dialectic, "conceptual collectivization," and (in theory at least) the moral justification of the dictatorship of the proletariat.

More moderate was the Achdut Ha'avoda (Unity of Labor) movement, which was known in that period as "Faction 'B' " and which was led by Yitzhak Tabenkin. This group adopted the theory of Marxism, and although its ideological link with the Soviet Union was close, it was a "selective" link, distinguishing between the good and the deficient aspects of the Soviet State. Among its younger leaders and spokesmen, besides Yisrael Galili, was Yoska Rabinowitz.

The debate was concerned not only with Marxism versus Democratic Socialism in general, but also with the future of the country. Meir Yaari and Yakov Hazan, the leaders of the Hashomer Hatzair, stood for a binational state. Tabenkin, who stood for the integrity of western Eretz Israel, preferred an international mandate over the entire area, so as to prevent its partition. On the other hand, Ben-Gurion's thoughts were developing in the direction of the "Biltmore Program," which provided for the immediate creation of a Jewish State, even at the price of the partition of Eretz Israel.

The debate was complex, and there were those who saw themselves as Marxists in social policy but supporters of Biltmore in regard to Zionist politics. And conversely, there were ideological Social Democrats who were politically in favor of the integrity of Eretz Israel. With the latter was Berl Katznelson, who still disagreed with Ben-Gurion's acceptance of partition.

The heart of the Youth Movement was shortly divided. Once, when we needed to prepare a declaration for May Day, there was a stormy argument over whether to include the word "immediate" in the section concerning a Jewish State, or to omit this word and "State" as well, since this could imply acceptance of the idea of partition. These topics were also discussed in the seminar, but with emphasis on the ideological aspect: Marxism versus Democratic Socialism.

The case for Marxism was put by a speaker who held his audience enthralled: Yoska Rabinowitz from Naan. He was then a young man, tall with a pale, finely chiseled face and a mass of tousled black hair. Yoska spoke with compelling logic and great persuasiveness. His speech was fairly long, and from time to time he would address himself to what were apparently side issues, with the object of relieving the tension by discussing topics of more widespread cultural interest.

For example, in one such aside he described his visit to the Rodin Museum in Paris. He described each piece of sculpture, telling us how the marble had submitted to the hands of the artist, and how Rodin had transformed the image of an old woman into an object of great beauty; he also described the pair of lovers that make up the sculpture entitled "Eternal Spring," telling us how it really was possible to sense the blood flowing in the veins of their marble limbs.

Yoska spoke for three days running, each day being divided equally between lecture and discussion. Berl was present all the time, his disheveled head cupped in his hands. Like most men of the Second Aliyah, Berl had a remarkable gift for concentration, equally able to absorb both the written and the spoken word.

I still have the notebook in which I recorded at the time the excitement aroused in me by Yoska's address. On the first page Marx's dictum is inscribed in large letters: "Wise men have interpreted the world differently; the vital thing is—to change it!"

The aim of Yoska's lectures was to prove that Marxism was the newest and highest of the sciences and that every forward-looking person must obey it and act in accordance with its dictates. According to him, the world of science had been enriched by a new branch, Marxist sociology, which like every scientific teaching was based on causation, not on theology. Sociology had taken the place of theology. "The mole," Yoska explained, "has eyes to see in the dark. Theology asks: 'What is the purpose of such eyes?' and replies, 'In order to see in the dark.' The new science asks, 'For what reason does the mole have such eyes?' and of course the answer is, *'in order to become accustomed to the dark.'* Theology is obliged to ask the question, 'Why does the universe exist?' A question posed in such a form demands a religious answer, 'In order to serve God, to obey a Higher Authority . . .' Whereas the new science examines in detail the causes that have led to the development of the universe, thus creating the potential to bring about further developments. From this it follows that the study of causation opens the way to the improvement of that which exists."

All of the audience, myself included, felt that we were on the side of modern science, not of antiquated theology.

Subsequently, Yoska described the structure of the world of science: "At its base, at the mathematical level, lies the question: what is two plus two, which makes no distinction between four people and four apples. A higher level is physics, which recognizes the gravitational pull of the earth but takes no interest in the question of what is actually drawn toward it—moon or meteorite? The next stage is chemistry, which examines the quantitative constitution of matter and its classification, but is not concerned with its birth and development. These are supplemented by biology, which comes to grips with other questions such as the structure of inner cells, their proliferation and growth. And recently a new science has been developed—psychology, which demands to know the connection between the mind and the body."

But even with all these sciences, it was still not possible to explain all phenomena, especially social phenomena. "These sciences are quite incapable of explaining the outbreak of the French Revolution, for example, or the birth of the kibbutz." From this it followed that we needed a new science, higher and more advanced, a science concerned with the laws of causation governing social phenomena. Such a science was gradually being born: in 1845 Robert Meyer's book on energy appeared, which claims that energy can never cease to exist; 1857 saw the publication of Charles Darwin's book, explaining the evolution of life and development through the survival of the fittest. And in the same year appeared Karl Marx's study of political economy, which insists that social and political change have their roots in *economic* factors.

This brought us round to Marxism. And Yoska spoke out firmly against the opponents of Marx's teaching. Some people refuse to accept Marxism because Marx was concerned with the true fundamental causes of the problems rather than with imaginary short-term solutions and because he proved conclusively that it is also the methods of production that determine the direction of political and cultural life. The ruling classes detested Marxism because, as far as they were concerned, it demanded the destruction of the entire ideological base on which their power and profits depended.

The longer the lectures continued, the more convinced we became. Suddenly we understood everything perfectly, all the causes and laws of existence, and we too felt ourselves part of a progressive world. I fear that we would have remained loyal Marxists to the end of our lives, had not Berl sensed that all this would lead to a divergence in the world view of the Socialist Zionist movement of Eretz Israel.

Berl gave his reply in a series of lectures that lasted nearly thirty hours. His lectures were arranged in the style of informal conversation, in which he addressed himself both to comments made from the floor of the debate and to the words of the principal speaker. Although his audience consisted of some forty to fifty young people, he treated this audience as if it were a great and influential crowd, whose opinions mattered. He never showed a moment's impatience or the slightest sign of urgency. He gave us the impression that he attached the very highest importance to the seminar. It was obvious that he was trying very hard to speak plainly and intelligibly, and his style of lecturing made his words easily digestible, in spite of their erudition. To make his message more agreeable he brought in a number of jokes. For example, when commenting on Hashomer Hatzair's misgivings about uniting with Mapai he told the story of a girl who was afraid to marry her fiancé, "because he's a stranger." And when her mother told her that when she married her husband he too was a stranger, the girl answered: "Yes, but that was my father. . . ."

Berl used a great many quotations; in fact he turned quotation into an art form in its own right. At the end of the series of lectures, Berl showed me, at my request, his system for preparing quotations. From everything that he read—books, newspapers, magazines—and from everything that he heard—conversations, lectures, chance encounters—he would make notes on a special card. He indexed these cards according to subject—revolution, bureaucracy, liberty, dictatorship, etc., and in preparation for the lecture that he was about to give, he would pick out the cards under the appropriate headings. He arrived for the lectures at Ben-Shemen armed with about a hundred of these cards. He quoted Yurgenev and Brenner, Herzen and Lassalle, Clara Zetkin and Rosa Luxemburg, Karl Liebknecht and Kropotkin, Ab Cohen and Isar Kochowsky, and many more. And naturally he often quoted from the Bible—Isaiah, Jeremiah, Job and Proverbs.

In the lectures themselves there were two quite distinct approaches: one of them personal and very subjective, arising from his deep disillusionment with the Russian Revolution and with what had come about in a land that had always been dear to him. It should be remembered that besides Jewish and Hebrew culture, the encouragement of which was a lifelong preoccupation for him, Russian culture was also close to his heart and served as a broad and sensitive backdrop to his intellectual experience. Like all those of the Second Aliyah, Berl was devoted to this culture. He lived it, followed it, fought it, and because of his love of it was deep and emotional, his disillusionment with it was equally deep and more painful than he cared to reveal to us.

The other approach was that of a teacher, devoting consistent and sensitive efforts to saving us from the fatal charms of Bolshevism. He also knew that we did not have the same broad grounding in Russian culture and that what little we knew of it and about it was through the medium of translation or from people who compared it unfavorably with other cultures. When he mentioned the name of Belinsky, or a concept such as the reallocation of land to the peasants, he was obliged to elucidate. In matters such as this Berl proved himself an incomparable teacher.

His lectures were marked by an additional quality: he did not present us with ready-made conclusions, he did not feed us cooked meat, whose merit consists solely in its packaging. He dismantled every line of thought to its smallest components, shedding light on them and inviting us to examine the nuts and bolts for ourselves and to work out how they operated.

Berl's was a *censorious* temperament. His criticisms were aimed in all directions, both outward and inward. It was not for nothing that he chose for himself the nickname "Jerububaal"—he had no time for idolatry or superstition of any kind. His censorious instinct was also reflected in the titles of his articles: for example, *In Favour of Confusion and Against Whitewash* * or *Even in Laughter the Heart is Sad.*† He tended to use double negatives as a substitute for direct unequivocal affirmation. And

---

* The title implies that he would prefer to be a confused Social Democrat than a whitewashed Marxist.

† This title means that, even if one takes the orientation towards the USSR lightly, it is still sad to think that in a free society there are people who would willingly follow it.

when he expressed a negative, he did not hesitate to destroy the corresponding affirmative, or what was mistakenly taken to be an affirmative.

In the introductory remarks to his lectures he said: "The great strength of all socialist thinkers consists in examination of the social order. This also applies to the sayings of the Prophets. While a small element of prophecy is concerned with foretelling the future, the bulk of it is made up of reproof and accusation directed toward negative phenomena. How can we appreciate the idealism of Isaiah son of Amoz, if we do not know what it was that provoked his anger?"

The gist of Berl's speeches at the seminar has been published in a small book entitled *Hidden Values*. (In describing the content of his remarks I shall have recourse both to extracts from this book—presented within quotation marks—and to my own memories.) Although the book gives a faithful record of Berl's main points, it cannot convey the spirit of his words. I recall the lectures as a mixture of ferocious polemic and grim analysis of the Bolshevik experiment in Soviet Russia. Berl disposed of many preconceptions and his intellectual broom left no hidden corner unswept. This was a challenge both to theory and its implementation, since the test of theory is implementation.

"The world does not exist on a *tabula rasa,* we are not born outside history," said Berl, "but political education means, in my view, certain values, both national and cultural, which should be the property of every generation." This was the preface to his fundamental claim—that the Bolshevik Revolution had demolished almost all the values to which it supposedly adhered. It had worked in a manner quite contrary to all expectations, and to the powerful wind that had originally filled its sails. Not only was there scant resemblance between Bolshevik ideals and the Bolshevik reality, they were diametrically opposed.

"A man joins the Socialist movement because he has ideas about wrong and injustice and he wishes to set the crooked straight; alas for the Socialist party that has lost the power to distinguish between disease and cure and adds wrongdoing to injustice." Socialism, said Berl, aspires "to take power out of the hands of the capitalist class and hand it over to the *people.*" It abhors the authority of man over man, although to a certain extent this was inevitable, since "Socialism means the *advancement of man,*" and it deplores the authority of nation over nation. In support of this he quoted Marx's own words: "A nation that enslaves another is forging its own chains."

Berl took issue with the concept of the "dictatorship of the proletariat" and with deprivation of personal freedom. "It is true," he said, "that the dictatorship of the proletariat is a concept susceptible to different interpretations. But is it really possible to arrive at freedom through nonfreedom, at nonviolence through violence?" Anyone who thinks that dictatorship is only a transitional phase on the way to political and economic democracy, must provide an answer to the question: "How will dictatorship give way to another system?" It is hardly to be expected that "dictatorship will abrogate itself, out of its own goodwill." Dictatorship of the proletariat is in fact dictatorship of the central committee. "Is it not impossible," insisted Berl, "for every comrade to have a say in this dictatorship?" Furthermore, a central committee of a hundred and fifty members is too large to impose an effective dictatorship, so power passes into the hands of the political committee. But in the political committee disagreements and personal rivalries arise, and then a less formal body is created, a "septemvirate" or a "quinquevirate" or a "triumvirate" and ultimately power rests in the hands of one man, the leader.

"Such a leader may be a savior or an angel, but he may equally well be a very simple man—simple and cruel." Here Berl quoted with an ironical smile a remark of Chaim Greenberg, who once said that he would be prepared to take on the yoke of a dictatorship on the condition that this was the dictatorship "of one man—the Messiah King," and this not only because the Messiah King was "girded with justice" but because *he had not yet come!*

The use of the word "proletariat" in conjunction with "dictatorship" is no cause for consolation. What does "rule by the workers" really mean? "Does a workers' government exist when the head of state is himself of the working class?" After all, "the Berlin housepainter," Adolf Hitler, was both a worker and a proletarian, and the same applies to Mussolini, who was the son of a blacksmith and trained as a primary school teacher.

There is no value in Socialism if freedom is denied, equal freedom for every man. There can be no Socialism without democracy, and autocracy undermines the very essence of Socialism. Bolshevism has established a permanent dictatorship, given privileges to the governing class, created a vast gap in living standards and poured scorn on equality, for which it has substituted repression and violence.

Such was Berl's detailed and ruthless analysis of the Communist revolutionaries and of the way in which they betrayed the principles that they had espoused, the moment they came to power. And he went on to examine these principles one by one:

THE SANCTITY OF HUMAN LIFE

In *Spartakusbriefe* (the newspaper of the early German Communists) Rosa Luxemburg wrote: "The proletariat revolution needs no terror for the attainment of its ends. It detests, it deplores any form of homicide." At the beginning of their campaign the revolutionaries promised to abolish the death penalty. But not only was the sword unsheathed, it began cutting off heads indiscriminately—sometimes including their own. "What is the use of purification after death?" asked Berl sarcastically. "Nobody comes back from there!"

"Men who were admired yesterday, were taken

out and executed today, and the man who was a hero the day before yesterday became a traitor over- night." And men were put to death not because of crimes they had committed but on account of dis- agreement, suspicion, accusation or informing. Even the murder of Trotsky, perpetrated outside the bor- ders of Russia by agents of Stalin, even that passed without undue foment in the Communist world. And since then the sword had spared few of the plan- ners and activists of the revolution.

ABOLITION OF PRIVATE PROPERTY

The denial of freedom was explained as being nec- essary for the achievement of economic equality. The same reasoning was applied to nationalization. But had the abolition of private property really brought equality and prosperity to the citizens of Russia? "The pyramids of Egypt," said Berl, "were not private property but the property of the State— how did the working man who built them benefit from the project?" If private property has not been replaced by freedom and equality but by tyranny on the part of the state, what point has been served by its abolition? A state can be no less tyrannical than a class.

RELIGIOUS FREEDOM

In the intellectual scheme drawn up by Karl Marx, a scheme to which he attached great importance, one of the provisions states that "all groups and individuals belonging to it (the International) must decide what is true, just and moral on the basis of the links which are shared by all humanity, without regard to race, religion or nationality." And even Lenin wrote, added Berl, that if a priest wished to join the party he should be admitted like any other man, according to the Socialist principle that "religion is a matter of personal conscience." But in the reality of Soviet life the opposite had happened. Russia had begun persecuting people on religious grounds and atheism had become the exclusive authority, a kind of nonreligion, the most fanatical of all faiths.

NATIONAL FREEDOM

As early as 1901, *Iska,* the mouthpiece of the Russian Social Democrats, had stated that "all of us, citizens of Russia, must take note of the disgrace that threatens us. We are still slaves in the sense that we are being used for the enslavement of other peoples, to hold them in a state of serfdom. We are still forced to endure an authority which not only represses with the hangman's ferocity any aspiration toward freedom in Russia, but also uses the Russian army to violate the freedom of others." Who would have imagined that these harsh words, which at that time were directed against the Czarist regime, would continue to be appropriate and applicable to the writers themselves? In this context Berl mentioned the conquest of Finland by Soviet Russia in 1939. And what would Berl have said about events of a later period, the violent subjugation of Hungary,

Poland and Czechoslovakia, at the hands of the Red Army? Berl had no sympathy for the view that the executioner of a workers' state is somehow different from the executioner of a bourgeois state. "An executioner is an executioner," was his acid comment.

FREEDOM OF STUDY

Berl quoted the Prussian Minister of Education, Bouse, who said in the Parliament of his country, in May 1897, that "you cannot kill ideas with artillery" and then told us about Reisenov, the greatest Marxist scholar in Soviet Russia, who was dismissed from the Marxist-Leninist Government in Moscow and even exiled to Siberia, for expressing his satisfaction, in retrospect, at the breach that had opened at the beginning of this century between the Mensheviks and the Bolsheviks. Scientific research, literature and art—all these had been suppressed in the Soviet Union and brought under the supervision of the Politburo, an institution whose members are not necessarily devotees of objective scientific research or men remarkable for their literary taste and artistic vision. Marxism, supposedly the champion of science, had become a chain binding the hands of scholars and artists.

OPEN DIPLOMACY

When he was Foreign Minister, Trotsky promised that revolutionary Russia would eschew secret diplomacy, which hides the truth from the people and nourishes strife and contention among nations. This promise too was ground into the dust. Soviet diplomacy had become one of the most mysterious and secret diplomacies of all, a diplomacy which did not hesitate to adopt the most dishonorable and violent means.

THE NATURE OF THE MARXIST STATE

In this connection Berl quoted from a philosopher who said: "Supposing that you need to bake a ton of bread. If you take a ton of dynamite and try to bake bread by the heat of the explosion—the results are not encouraging and the bread is inedible anyway. . . ." He also turned for support to one of the greatest Communists, Rakovsky, who wrote from his place of exile in Siberia: "We are building a workers' State that is crippled by bureaucracy . . . a bureaucratic State with only the tattered relics of proletarian Communism. It has created, and it is still creating, a huge class of dictators, in which there is an internal hierarchy dividing the high from the low." In Berl's view, the true test of Marxist theory was the regime based on the teaching of Marx and Engels.

In this regime, what had happened to the advancement of man, his culture, his equality, his relationship with others? What had become of revolutionary truth, of its redeeming force? "The whole of the great ideal," said Berl, "foundered primarily on the weakness of its disciples." It was the weakness of the disciples that had sealed the fate of the Communist ideal in Soviet Russia.

The impact of these lectures was deep and decisive. I believe that these, and similar lectures heard in other places, left an indelible impression on many of us. They implanted in us a negative attitude toward the Communist revolution and Marxist dialectic, an attitude more interested in the values of the human race than in the study of Soviet Russian statistics. These lectures brought us back from the *Communist Manifesto* to the vision of the Prophets.

Berl devoted a considerable part of these lectures to matters concerning the Labor movement in Eretz Israel. Berl was most censorious and full of concern at what was happening to the image and ideals of the Labor movement. He was worried about recent developments within the framework of the movement and was convinced that unity would increase its strength whereas factionalism would sow hatred and cause weakness. He was faced with the dilemma that confronts every workers' movement: how to create, on the one hand, an acceptable compromise, a shared program, as a basis for the consolidation of a large body of opinion; on the other hand, how to ensure that compromise for tactical purposes does not become compromise of essential principle.

Berl coined the slogan "Liberty of thought and unity of action" as a basis for the organization of the Labor movement. But he was well aware that the workers' movements would divide not only according to political orientations or ideological viewpoints but also on account of the plethora of organizational forms and policy systems.

Berl was afraid of compromise in the ideological sphere. He saw in the debate with the Communist standpoint a continuation of the debate that had accompanied the Jewish people for generations: the struggle against assimilation, Hellenization and self-deprecation of the individual. His fear was that imported Socialism might bring about religious and national apostasy, thereby destroying the Zionist and democratic base of the Labor movement in Eretz Israel. But he was no more inclined toward excessive compromise in the organizational sphere; with all his vigor he strove for the unity of the Labor movement, for genuine unity, and he utterly abhorred the formation of factions and blocs. He saw factionalism as a malignant disease capable of destroying all that was good in the movement, as a breeding ground for intrigue, strife, bitterness and suspicion, an atmosphere in which one faction is constantly undermining another, one man is constantly undermining his comrade, and each individual is constantly undermining his own personal integrity.

I had experience of this dilemma myself while still a young man. I was a member of the secretariat of Hanoar Haoved, a youth organization that had been born in Eretz Israel and was wide-embracing in its structure and united in its viewpoint. But in practice the movement was under the almost sole influence of "Faction 'B' " (or Achdut Ha'avoda). Ten out of the twelve members of the secretariat were members of "Faction 'B'," representing the United Kibbutz Movement; the other two, Nahman Raz and I, belonged to Mapai, representing the Settlements Association.

The Settlements Association (which today is the Union of Kibbutzim and Settlements) advocated small, intimate communities—as opposed to the concept of the large kibbutz favored by Lavie and Tabenkin—and it was subject to the influence of the "Gordonia" movement, which had a youth organization of its own. "Gordonia," as is well known, followed the teaching of A. D. Gordon, a teaching which is the reverse of Marxism: work is "religious" since man may be redeemed by it; there can be no equality unless it is bound up with liberty, and there can be no Socialism unless it is humane. This movement also abhorred the symbols of International Socialism—the Red Flag, May Day, and the very word "Socialism."

Hanoar Haoved did not dictate ideas and it was open to all. It strove to establish a broad framework which would absorb all the various currents and avoid the generation of negative energy, which breeds internecine hatred. (Nathan Alterman used to make fun of our earnest debates, saying: "The Jews are so mean that if they begin to hate each other, it has to be hatred for nothing. . . .") The influence of Achdut Ha'avoda over Hanoar Haoved threatened its unity and the separate existence of

"Gordonia" threatened its wholeness. It was necessary, anyway, to fight on two fronts: to open up Hanoar Haoved to all shades of opinion, especially to those who rejected the authority of Achdut Ha'avoda, and to draw members of the Settlements Association into Hanoar Haoved, with the ultimate aim of making the two organizations one. In this campaign I worked under Berl's guidance.

At the congress of Hanoar Haoved, held in 1943, there was a sensational surprise. In the congress two lists were canvassing: the "Benjamin List" (named after Benjamin Hachlili of Achdut Ha'avoda, a member of the secretariat and of Kibbutz Naan), and the "Shimon List" (named after me but in fact a Mapai manifesto). Contrary to all expectations the "Shimon Memorandum" won an absolute majority in the congress.

Berl was delighted. At the same time he was concerned lest the victory prove to be a Pyrrhic one, leading to the disintegration of the movement. After many tense hours, and with the support of David Cohen, "the Father of Hanoar Haoved," we did in fact arrive at an agreement between the two factions, thus preserving the unity of our movement, at the price of providing for informal "parity" in its institutions. But this was only half the battle. Now we had to bring "Gordonia" into Hanoar Haoved.

I traveled around the organization's farms, persuading the young people to lend their support to the unity of the movement, at least at the level of the younger generation. Berl followed my efforts closely, and he knew every trick in the game. I agreed with him that we should organize a conference of the Settlements Association at which an announcement would be made of the integration of Hanoar Haoved into the Histadrut. Berl promised to be the principal speaker at this conference. We fixed a date and a venue—Kibbutz Alumot.

A few days before the conference was due to open, Berl summoned me to his house. I found him pale, wrapped up in himself and suffering, as usual, from headaches. I also sensed that he was embarrassed and finding great difficulty in opening a conversation. After a short silence he said: "I promised you that I would take part in the conference and make a speech. And I really meant it. But in the meantime something had happened which has upset my intention. A few days ago there was a meeting of the Party Secretariat at which Pinhas Lavon [the leader of "Gordonia"] violently attacked the holding of the conference and claimed that it would not be a conference of unity but a conference of disintegration. He added that he had heard that I was due to take part in it and to be the principal speaker. If this was really true, he saw it as an act of hostility toward his movement, and he intended to draw his own conclusions."

Berl paused, thought for a moment and went on: "It is not in our interests to endanger the integrity of the party, yet we must not interrupt the campaign for unity—unity which will begin with the young generation. You carry on anyway with the organization of the conference and don't call it off. It is vital for our future. But I cannot take part in it."

His words shocked me deeply; the sudden disappointment struck me like a bolt from the blue. And I was grieved that such pressure had been brought to bear on Berl and that he had been forced to submit to it. Hurriedly I took leave of Berl and returned to my room, thoroughly demoralized, but also more mature: I knew the true meaning of disappointment, disappointment imposed by external pressures.

Berl was aware of my disappointment, and soon afterward he made a conciliatory suggestion: at a later date, after the conference, he would visit Alumot to talk with the members. He arrived on the eve of Passover, and the first thing that he asked to see was a modern version of the Passover Haggadah, which the members of the community had composed.

Two marvelous extracts from Berl's own writings had been incorporated into this Haggadah: "Passover, a people celebrating over two thousand years the day of its deliverance from slavery: through all the depths of enslavement and oppression—the Inquisition, annihilation and pogroms—the nation has kept alive its common yearnings for freedom from which not one Jewish soul shall be excluded. On every soul lies the weight of oppression and degradation! From fathers to sons, throughout all generations, the story of the Exodus from Egypt has been passed on as a personal memory that neither pales nor fades. In every generation, the Jew must feel as if *he himself came out from Egypt.* You will find no more exalted consciousness of history than this, no greater commingling of the individual and the group—in the breadth of the world and the depth of time—than that expressed in the ancient lesson which we are commanded to teach our children. I know of no work of literature more conducive to an abhorrence of serfdom and a love of liberty than the story of bondage in Egypt and the Exodus. And I know of no ancient memory more directed toward the future, more indicative of our today and our tomorrow, than the memory of the Exodus from Egypt."

Kibbutz Alumot lies on the flank of a hill in lower Galilee. It looks out over an exhilarating panorama of the Sea of Galilee and the Jordan Valley. Every ray of the sun gives a different shade of the Jordan as it meanders through the valley, colors ranging from a seductive green to an aristocratic silver. The whole landscape spoke of spring, a gentle breeze caressing the fields still overflowing with green shoots. Berl reveled in these scenes, gazing down toward the settlement at Kinneret, below Alumot, where he had spent perhaps the happiest period of his life. He sat down on the grass, leafed through the Haggadah and said: "I don't care for modern versions of the Haggadah. It may be that new expressions are to some extent appropriate to our times, but they detract from the primeval historical force. Words are not born in the dictionary.

The dictionary confirms them. It is the *past* that gives them content and meaning."

Berl told me that he never touched pork, not only because it was forbidden in the law, but also out of respect to those Jews who refused to obey the orders of their oppressors and preferred to die rather than eat forbidden food. This too was a form of rebellion, rebellion of the few against the many, of independent people against their conquerors, a rebellion no less important than the greatest rebellions known to man. He also said that he always fasted on Yom Kippur and the ninth of Ab. I found the explanation for this among his writings: "Israel has always kept its day of mourning, the day of the loss of its freedom. And on this day (the ninth of Ab), in every generation, the Jew sees *himself* as the man whose world is in ruins."

Berl's attachment to tradition was permanent and deep. He wanted to make it the property of the entire movement. He said. "A generation that renews and creates things from scratch must under no circumstances reject the legacy of past generations. What is needed is to restore the ancient tradition of life and use it to strengthen this progressive generation. If in the life of our people there is something very old and deep, which has the power to educate —would it not be a tragic mistake to reject it?"

"The Jewish year," Berl wrote in another place, "is thickly sown with days of far deeper significance than anything to be found in the calendars of other peoples. Is it the concern for the function of the

Jewish Labor movement to waste the strength stored up in them?

"Is Socialism—the ideal of liberty in labor—favorable to religion, tolerant of religion, or inimical to religion?" In reply to this almost rhetorical question, Berl posed another: "Is this a movement of faith or of apostasy?" He took up arms against the "subjective perception" of "some of the greatest Socialists, who seek to turn us into a church with priests and preachers, but an Epicurean church." He believed that this approach was doing great damage both to the ideology and the public image of the Socialist movement.

"Seeing that our Socialism is not made of paper but is practical, can we expect the Yemenite Jew to build his life on an Epicurean foundation; can we demand of him loyalty to the working class alone?" And Berl added: "The members of Hapoel Hamizrachi (Religious Workers' Party) are, in my view, good workers and loyal pioneers, as well as being pious by nature. Are we to say to them: 'First of all you must convert to our atheistical religion?'? Or perhaps we should say: 'You can be faithful to your religion, and our loyal comrades as well.' "

Berl's guiding principle was that: "Those who seek to build a country cannot do so through hired labor but the energy and resources of the whole people must be mobilized." Policy should be directed toward the maximum concentration, and confusion of political with religious debate should be carefully avoided. Berl did not advocate the abandonment of freedom of conscience on the part of any man or movement. On the contrary: "Spiritual reflection and intellectual consideration are an obligation." And as usual, Berl derived support in this context from literary sources. Commenting that in the works of Azar there were "sparks of true Socialism," he quoted him as saying that "from youths of the yeshiva Jewish Socialism shall grow."

In his evaluation of religion Berl disagreed absolutely with the Marxist doctrine that "religion is the opium of the people." In Berl's view religion was history and as such a guide to the future. He used to insist that a Socialism that does not make allowances for the Jewish immigrant worker from the Yemen, and does not know what conditions are like for the Jewish minority in the Yemen, ignores both the fate of the Zionist movement and the character of the Labor movement.

Berl liked to describe himself as a man of strife and contention, the scourge of his compatriots. And he really was a remarkable polemicist. He preferred the system of debate, usually with others but sometimes even with himself, as the best method of elucidating things. He argued over issues but he also argued with people. With his "devastating" intellect" (as Alterman called it) Berl was capable of vanquishing any opponent. It is enough to look at his attack on the Hashomer Hatzair in his two articles *In Favour of Confusion and Against Whitewash* and *Even in Laughter the Heart is Sad*, to see how he turned polemic into an art. And sometimes it seemed that Berl was charged with an electrical force, capable of penetrating masks, exposing weakness and discovering vulnerable points.

Like Ben-Gurion he saw untruth as the root cause of the tragedy of self-delusion, the altar on which so many of our people have fallen. He attacked careerism and careerists in violent terms and he was opposed to bureaucracy, which paves the way to dissension and degeneracy. He chose his targets with care and did not miss.

Sometimes the depth of his pessimism worried me. He used to speak of the foreseeable future with convincing gloom. He was afraid that the pillars of our world might suddenly collapse through a fundamental weakness, like the pillars of the Philistine temple that fell on the head of the blind Samson.

Was it his intention to uproot every weed in our fields? Or was he perhaps afraid that our soil was capable of producing no more grass? Was he like Jeremiah, lamenting the destruction that is imminent, or like Isaiah, saying, "Comfort ye, comfort ye my people"? There were elements of both in him, but he was always incisive and uncompromising in regard to the truth.

Berl loved literature but he did not have the confidence to be a writer. He took up his pen with a mixture of enthusiasm and fear. For this reason the greater part of his teaching was oral. He disseminated knowledge and he challenged it, he caused changes and upheavals and he prevented unwanted changes and unnecessary sensations. He sought to unite the glories of our past and our present-day needs together in one unique path, a path in which we might walk without betraying our heritage and without compromising our identity.

He played the role of a midwife to industry, and he was the educator of many people in all walks of life. He was a focus—a central source of light and of heat, heat both to warm and to scorch. From David Ben-Gurion people expected vision, conclusions and decisions. They went to Berl to pour out their hearts, to confide, to ask for advice and reassurance.

Of course, the movement is not only a formal framework for the shaping and implementation of policies. It is also a human arena, a beehive of people full of honey and stings, always throbbing and bristling, complex and riddled with contradictions. Hand in hand with enthusiasm and faith go notoriety, suspicion, mistrust and doubt. No one was as aware as Berl of the *human* element in the movement, of the greatness and frailty of the individual.

People were drawn to him like moths to a flame: for an understanding of things, for encouragement, for the discovery of their latent creative potential. Berl would listen with endless patience, with true attentiveness, separating the wheat from the chaff, diagnosing weaknesses and giving support where required, determining the rungs on the ladder of priorities, soothing strife, spurring people on to think more and to think more positively and to learn unceasingly.

He did not accept the conventional distinction

between small things and great, young men and old, the rank and file and the leadership—all were important and worthy of arousing his curiosity. His literary tastes were similarly wide; he read everything—classic novels and minor articles in youth newspapers, the first fruits of young authors and critical studies of ancient Hebrew writings. He revealed the greatness in small things. Everything that grows has first been planted somewhere, and the seed must be understood as well as the fruit.

Berl was the teacher of a generation. A teacher in the highest and broadest sense of the word. And when I saw the crowds who accompanied him on his last journey, I knew that these were the people whom Berl had accompanied on their first journey.

NATHAN ALTERMAN
The Poet—His Best Poem

*I shall not cease to watch and I shall not cease to breathe
and when I die I shall go on walking.*

NATHAN ALTERMAN

I REMEMBER a conversation that took place one day between Ben-Gurion, Nehemiah Argov and myself about Nathan Alterman. Ben-Gurion asked a lot of questions—what was he writing now, from where was he drawing his literary resources, what did he intend to publish, had his writings been collected, was his livelihood secure? We told Ben-Gurion that Nathan was living, and working, in a modest and cramped apartment in a noisy Tel Aviv street; we did not know what he was writing or where it was

153

to be published; he was hiding himself away, leading a lonely and inscrutable life.

This was in the early 1950s. The government was then engaged in the building of housing projects to accommodate civil servants and Regular Army soldiers, and in fact many apartments were still vacant and were on offer to any applicant. We were struck by the idea of offering the poet a more spacious lodging in a quieter corner, so that he could work undisturbed by the noise of the traffic at the intersection of Nordau Boulevard and Dizengoff Street.

We talked to Nathan and explained the offer, stressing that he would not be receiving any kind of preferential treatment and that he would be expected to pay the full rent.

Nathan was most moved; our sympathy astonished him. And when Nathan was moved, he used to stammer. He had difficulty replying, but from his expression we could tell that something about our suggestion was not to his liking. Finally he managed to say that he could not give an immediate reply, but that if we met again the following day, he would then have an answer for us.

We met the following day, and once again he had difficulty expressing himself. After a while he produced a sheet of paper and read the following statement:

> I am very grateful to you for your offer. I know that your motives are sincere. I be-

lieve your assurance that I will be able to continue criticizing David Ben-Gurion. But after careful consideration I have arrived at a negative decision. It is true that it takes courage to criticize. But *praising* the man, *speaking in his favor*—how could I do that living in an apartment which he and you had helped me to obtain . . . ?

At a party celebrating Ben-Gurion's eightieth birthday, we persuaded Nathan to make a speech. Among other things, he said: "It is in the nature of truth to stand on the side of the man whose cause is just."

Nathan was convinced that Ben-Gurion's cause was just, and that the truth stood on his side. He wanted to be at liberty to give his support to the man of just cause; he wanted to be free to do this, since he could never allow himself to evade the truth, however controversial the truth might be. And he knew very well that as a man of popular esteem—"the brightest jewel of our poetry, its quiet and noble pride"—his words carried weight and authority; it was therefore his duty to be free to praise and free to reprove, in speech, in allegory or in poetry.

In poetry there is "a union of passion and artistry, the melody of the strings and the mason's chisel." Emotional passion must be matched with sober reflection, the soaring melody with the chisel that fashions the image, creations of light and shade, praise and reproof, construction and contradiction, and he wanted to be a union of passion and reason, independent in his thinking, plucking his strings as he pleased, and sculpting his images according to his own designs.

Nathan loved his freedom and he guarded it jealously. He saw it as a part of his great responsibility. Chaim Hazaz characterized the poetry of Alterman most aptly, in the following terms: ". . . positive judgment of eternal truths, and the logic of the universe, enriched with deeds and exploits, order restraining the wickedness of mankind, the lyrical prayers of a man appealing to his Creator against the cruelty of fate." And Hazaz added that this poetry was "an opening of the eyes, a battle-cry burdened by suffering, a *poetry of responsibility*—responsibility born of moral rectitude, of self-denial, of the poetic essence stored within the recesses of the soul."

I see this combination—of high moral responsibility and an aptitude for self-denial—as the key to the personality of Nathan Alterman. And while meeting Ben-Gurion always inspired in me a sense of exaltation, of a man capable of soaring to unknown heights, meeting Nathan would give me a feeling of depth, of a man capable of diving into the abyss and drawing up from its unexplored recesses new experiences and visions, voices and melodies of unprecedented clarity.

Responsibility on the one hand, and depth on the other, created great tension in him. In a certain sense, Nathan was afraid of himself. His wisdom was so penetrating that he could pursue an objective to the end and reveal that beyond the apparent end lay a further, more terrifying end, an infinite end. It was as if he set out to study the creation of the world in reverse—from the seventh to the first day: from "and He saw that it was good," from "the tree bearing fruit," from "the herb yielding seed," from the dominion of day and the dominion of night and the great whales—to primeval chaos, darkness on the abyss and the Spirit moving on the face of the waters. When Nathan arrived at the point where it was hard to distinguish between day and night, between land and sea, he would stop himself, and go no further. He was afraid that this backward journey might lead him to nihilism, to cynicism, to despair —beyond catastrophe.

If his wisdom was capable of plunging into depths, his poetry was the lifeline that prevented him from sinking. His poetry balanced his intellect: the poetry of a new morning mist against an ancient and corrosive wisdom, capable of making the opaque transparent, of turning matter into time. He entrusted to his poetry the most responsible of functions, a role of compensation and equilibrium, to dispel the despair at the brink of the abyss.

His attachment to the Hebrew language, to Hebrew poetry, was of a very special nature. It could indeed be said, in the words that Alterman himself used in a tribute to Shlonsky, that Hebrew was in love with him, like an amorous woman pursuing a man: "Hebrew is a little enamored of him . . . timo-

rous, yet lured on. . . ." She fell in love with him at
first sight, she did not leave him for a moment, and
wherever he went she followed—caressing him,
weaving fine garments for him, singing him the lov-
eliest tunes, refreshing his thirst, attending to all his
needs, both great and small; and he, sometimes in
untrammeled mischief, would try to elude her, to
explain to her that he was not a free man and he had
no taste for romance, he had in fact made a vow of
celibacy—he was a simple man, he loved simple
people and he wanted to live among them as a bach-
elor, not a family man; he had no aspiration toward
heroism, no wish to be admired, praised or flattered:

> I tried to tell her I was a kind of young goat,
> And at the touch of her finger my wool blazed
>   with joy.

He resisted her, but in the end he offered to
surrender, on the condition that she let him retain
his identity—the identity of a man of the people,
one in a multitude, a relation but not an overlord.

Nathan never wrote a proper will. He was not
the kind to devote painstaking effort to a purely personal matter; he regarded himself as a humble crea-
ture, whose most urgent needs could be simply and
frugally satisfied. Thus he lived, and thus he died.
Every word of his that was intended for publication,
he revised meticulously, time and again. But when
it came to a will, he was content with a rough draft,
containing a few simple words: he asked to be buried

"among ordinary Jews" and he did not want to be eulogized. Nathan not only loved "ordinary Jews"; he himself wanted to be "an ordinary Jew."

He was a wise man, a man of complexity and talent, capable of plunging deep into the regions where things are created, and yet he was afraid of this mystical aptitude and he tried, with the aid of his poetry, to stop himself at the point where things continue to exist. But his poetry, for its part, could not provide only the function of a brake; it developed a momentum of its own, flying off in new directions. Poetry played in him and through him tunes of charm and enchantment, while he, Nathan, strove hard to defend himself from their seductive delights, to be just a simple man, an ordinary Jew, modest of dress and frugal of diet, spontaneous in his joy and innocent in his sorrow.

He concealed his rich and unique world from the eyes of other people; he offered his friendship freely. A good companion, saying little and seeking refuge within his milieu, a companion without wealth, obligations or demands. A wanderer, giving support to the stumbling, consolation to the mourning, marveling at every human endeavor, attentive to every human mumble, intoxicated by every flower and drinking at the roadside fountain. "This man who walks within himself should not ask for rest and loneliness."

Nathan was always surrounded by friends. On one trip that we organized the party included Hannah Rovina, Avraham Halfi, Israel Zmora and Zev

Yoskovitz (Yosifon); on another trip he was joined by Rafael Eleaz, Moshe Shamir, Yoskovitz and Yani Avidov. Before every such trip, Nathan would gather together a group of people to whom he felt attached, people who interested or concerned him. There was a kind of inscrutable wisdom in his choice of friends: most of them were good at expressing themselves, all were lovers of poetry and music, people capable of being drawn toward the unexpected, concealing their love for Nathan and not forcing him to talk too much or to act as the central figure in the group.

This applied both to recreational trips and to expeditions undertaken for a specific purpose. On one occasion a group of people was assembled with the object of making sure that bomb shelters would be constructed in outlying settlements. The nucleus of the party, besides Nathan, consisted of Avraham Haft, Yani Avidov, and Zev Yoskovitz. I believe that on this occasion the project was the brainchild of Avraham Haft.

Haft, a member of Degania "B," was a man of remarkable vision and enthusiasm. He kept himself in a state of constant alert, on his guard against the weakness and complacency that lead men astray. His greatest fear was that in time of war, the aircraft that the Russians were supplying to Egypt would be directed against civilian targets, and that lacking proper shelters our settlements would suffer casualties. When Haft volunteered for the mission, he was immediately joined by Yani Avidov.

Like Haft, Yani was a man who abhorred routine. His imagination and his courage led him to accomplish the most impossible of missions. Once, accompanied by Ben-Zion Israeli, he slipped across the border into Iraq, crossed the desert and returned with a stock of date-palm cuttings, the origin of the trees which flourish today from Eilat to Tiberias. His book, *Iraqi Adventures*—written, I believe, at Nathan's instigation—is an enthralling account of a courageous pioneering mission. Avidov believed that great deeds spring from great dreams. According to him, dreaming was the essence of adventure, waking—a waste of energy and a loss of momentum.

And Yoskovitz accompanied Nathan wherever he went. In a dedication to Yoskovitz in *Tablet of the Land*, Nathan wrote:

> To Yoskovitz my lifelong friend and
>   companion,
> A man well versed in sweetness and strength,
> Who loves to make toasts with a glass of wine,
> And with a saying of Agnon or Hayyim Hazaz,
> Or a poem of the maestro (Shlonsky I mean),
> So to him this is offered, sealed and delivered,
> From his loyal and unswerving friend.

Yoskovitz's pockets were always crammed with papers bearing quotations from Yitzhak Manger, Kadia Molodovska and, naturally, from Alterman and Hazaz. He was fond of alcohol, and his cheeks were invariably red, from real or imaginary drinking;

any mission demanding action intoxicated him, and Nathan supplied this wine in generous doses. The three of them, one secretly and two openly, went around from door to door, from the Prime Minister's office to the homes of construction workers, urging, persuading, impressing upon all the need to build shelters, to prevent unnecessary injuries.

Other groups of people were mobilized by Nathan for "special purposes"—to help those in distress or bereavement. It is impossible to assess how much time and effort Nathan and his friends devoted to such cases of individual attention, sometimes even without the knowledge of the beneficiaries themselves. Nathan had a flair for choosing the right people to lend their support to such projects, people who would not be put off by the scorn of conventions or by the blank walls of bureaucracy. From time to time I myself was enlisted as a partner in such a group. An appeal from Nathan was not to be argued with; one simply had to identify with the causes that he espoused. The people and the causes were special indeed; they represented the exceptional—exceptional personalities, exceptional ideas. He admired such people and he was eager to help them.

There was the case of an actor who had all the qualities required of a great performer—enormous physical stature, a magnificent bass voice, a deep love of the theater and total dedication to the roles that he played. His dream was to play the part of King Lear, but every time that this dream came close to realization, some misfortune would befall the theater, or the production, or the man himself, and his hopes would be dashed once again. Finally he decided to form a theatrical company of his own, so that he would be able at last to take on the part of Shakespeare's tragic king. But here too he was unsuccessful. Before a single production could be mounted the theater collapsed for financial reasons, and he was forced to seek other employment.

Being a man of great physical strength, he found work as a building laborer. But his ill fortune followed him from the stage to the scaffolding. He injured his arm in an industrial accident and he was left without work and without livelihood. He decided to open a steak bar but the municipal authorities refused permission; in that area all the authorized places had already been allotted. Some of his friends mocked his misfortune, others smiled indulgently at his bizarre aspirations; one way or the other, they all deserted him. I do not know how he came into contact with Nathan, perhaps it was Nathan who discovered him. In any case, Nathan took up the man's case with all his warmth and energy. He trudged back and forth, appealing to the municipality, the police, the theater, to friends. It is true that he did not succeed in solving the man's problems—ultimately compassion proved powerless against the rigidity of entrenched bureaucracy—but to the end of his days he cherished the hope that a niche might be found for the unfortunate actor, and Nathan's sympathy was the only bright spot in the man's life.

And there was the case of the skipper—Nathan was always drawn towards sea captains—who also aspired to do something that ran counter to economic principle and conventional reckoning. The project, planned entirely on his own initiative, was to establish a shipping line between Eilat and Sharm-El-Sheikh. The enterprise was doomed from the start: there were no ports, no ships and no passengers. Since resources were lacking, he began the process of building up his "line" with the acquisition of a single ship. Furthermore, shortage of capital forced him to purchase a very antiquated ship, a ship that had been designed, and used for many years, as a pleasure steamer. It was easy to acquire such a ship, harder to operate it. A pleasure steamer is built on extravagant lines, for extravagant purposes; the cabins are spacious, the staterooms large and the engines consume vast quantities of fuel. The boat is designed only to accommodate a minimum of passengers wanting the maximum of fun. The ship was duly converted for its new role—and it limped all the way from Eilat to Sharm-El-Sheikh, with predictable and rapid results: all those who had once supported the idea of "the route," and "the shipping project," hurriedly washed their hands of the entire enterprise. And then the captain turned to Nathan.

Nathan sprang into action at once, full of enthusiasm. First of all, there was the man himself: a courageous seaman, one of the heroes of the illegal immigration in the period of the British Mandate, a man with a genuine sense of mission, not seeking profit for its own sake. Secondly, the place: Nathan had begun to cherish the dream of a Greater Israel, which would cover the whole of the Gulf of Eilat. Thirdly, the loneliness: all had turned their backs on the sea captain, leaving him stranded, alone with his inspiring dream on the deck of an obsolete ship. Nathan's imagination was set alight: a lonely skipper and a new route, a distant sea, a worn-out ship facing an impenetrable hinterland. . . . He set to work. He discovered institutions, departments, individuals and subsidies that nobody had even heard of, he made contacts, enticed them, soothed the vehemence of their opposition. After a while he approached the Ministry of Transport, in which at that time I was serving as Minister.

I explained to Nathan that one of the difficulties involved in operating this route was the problem of tying up the ship on the southern shore of Sharm-El-Sheikh, since the harbor had none of the facilities required for this, and the ship itself was too cumbersome to approach the shore under its own power. A few days later Nathan appeared in my office again, this time bringing a "document" that he had drawn up himself. The document included a bizarre illustration: passengers clambering ashore on a kind of rope ladder connecting the ship with the dry land. There were also detailed financial calculations, in foreign and local currency, to prove just how eminently feasible the project was; there was also a lyrical description of the kind of passenger for whom the opportunity to sail to the south would be the realization of a lifelong dream. . . .

I surrendered to this partnership of arch-admiral and arch-persuader, and the shipping line was put into operation. Later it emerged that the prose was more potent than the poetry and the dry land more realistic than the sea, and financial losses forced the closure of the line. But for a time, the seaman and the poet had shared the same dream.

In his dealings with the actor there was, of course, a reflection of the poet's attachment to the theater. Here was a strange man in a strange predicament, life and the stage linking arms to create a play within a play: while the actor still longed to act out the fate of a remote and ancient king, fate took a hand and cast him in a quite different role, not ancient but modern, a drama of alienation from those who had once been friends and admirers.

In Nathan's interest in the sea captain there was clearly an expression of his attachment to the sea, the great sea, apparently so pure, with its charming legends and ruthless ferocity. He hoped that the seaman would not be compelled to bow to the rules of the dry land. If only the land had provided the sea with a few paltry pennies, then the freshness of the dream need not have withered prematurely.

Of a quite different kind was Nathan's relationship with Bat-Miriam, the eminent poetess. Ever since her son fell in the Jerusalem hills in the War of Independence, Bat-Miriam had been dressed in mourning. Her tiny, almost miniature figure, her pale, delicate features and her manner of addressing people, always in the third person, created around her an air of reverence and mystery. She was invariably spoken of in hushed tones.

The celebrated Bat-Miriam belonged to no school, and she was a member of no group. She drew the inspiration for her poems from sources of her own, and her poetry has the taste of still waters from ancient wells. I experienced something of the flavor of her poetry at an early age. Berl Katznelson was one of her greatest admirers, and I still remember how he used to recite to me verses from her poem "Hagar":

> Alone, only she, the road,
> Blowing like a wind from the whiteness of
>   God,
> Like an inscription on parched earth,
> She set out with her child and her
>   loneliness. . . .

It seems that Berl and Nathan shared a love of her poetry. In later years I discovered that this love was mutual; in the collected edition of Bat-Miriam's works there are poems dedicated to Berl and to Nathan.

Nathan was much attracted by the individuality of the poetess, and he made himself responsible for the provision of her few needs. One of the services that he undertook on her behalf—which became known to me through hearsay—seems to exemplify all the delicacy implicit in his attachment to Bat-Miriam. Apparently, Nathan heard that she had great difficulty climbing stairs, and that in her house the distance between one step and the next was too much for her. He went out with his friends and collected a stock of books which he used to "carpet" the stairs, reducing the gap between them and enabling the poetess to climb up to her apartment without difficulty.

All such services performed by Nathan on her behalf were an expression of gratitude—gratitude for the refined loveliness of her poetry and gratitude to the poetess, who was a poet in her own right. This gratitude was also mutual. In her poem "Nathan Alterman," Bat-Miriam wrote:

> Only with him is her mind so sober and clear
> That it seems hesitant and wary.
> And he looks with wisdom and compassion
> On her innocence and elaborate cunning.

Nathan did not want to carve out his poems only from linguistic and literary sources, but also from the soil of experience. He longed to sing of reality. This is why he loved to travel, to measure distances, to touch things, to see life face to face. He devoted limitless energy to the recording of detail: the names of places and of people whom he met, the classification of the plants that he saw, the dates of events, the logic of things as observed through their creator. And he made copious and detailed preparations, both emotional and scholarly, before every one of his trips.

Nathan did not like committing himself in advance. If I were to invite him to join in a trip that was due to take place in a week's time, I knew what his reply would be: he would contact me the day before the trip, at the last moment; I had no doubt that he would accept the invitation, but he did not want to go around for a week feeling that he had committed himself to an engagement—a commitment that he might conceivably be prevented from honoring.

Nathan's manner and his style of dress were as undefinable as they were inimitable. There was nothing conventional about either. He wore a suit of indeterminate age, origin, and even color, except that it was dark rather than light. His shirt was buttoned up to the collar, even though he was not in the habit of wearing a tie. In his pocket he carried a pipe, which he would smoke from time to time, and large quantities of cigarettes; he also carried a leather satchel, of the kind used by schoolchildren, and since it was usually empty, I never understood what purpose it served. But I remember one occasion when it proved most useful.

In the course of our visit to Nahal-Yam, on the shores of the Bardawil lagoon, the fishermen insisted that Nathan take a fish home with him. They had difficulty persuading him, but after lengthy wrangling, I saw his eyes suddenly light up. He accepted the fish and put it into the empty briefcase with an expression of triumph, as if he had found the solution to an immensely complicated problem.

And on our return to Tel Aviv I saw him striding purposefully toward the house where Tirzah,* his daughter, lived. He was devoted to Tirzah and he was ready to do anything for her sake. In the poem that he addressed to her, there is a sense of premonition:

> Guard your soul, guard your strength, guard
> your soul,
> Guard your life, your understanding, guard
> your life,
> From a tottering wall, a burning roof, the
> shadows of night. . . .

During a trip he would ignore all inquiries as to whether he was hungry or thirsty, and it was hard to tell what kind of a mood he was in. His mood was as changeable as his poetry: sometimes solemn, sometimes mischievous, sometimes ironic, always introverted. There was no knowing whom he would choose as a traveling companion, but you could be sure that he would not come alone, that he would bring a friend. On these journeys he would occasionally depart from his habitual reticence, making remarks that sounded in themselves like poetry.

One day we were touring green and luscious plantations north of Tiberias. From time to time our jeep left the main road, and then we had a view of the Sea of Galilee from the other, unfamiliar side. It

---

* Tirzah was also a poet and, two years after her father's death, she met her own death by falling from a balcony.

was like standing on the dark side of the moon. Suddenly Nathan turned to me and said: "It seems that we are traveling behind the scenes of the State, seeing its abstract landscape."

In January 1960 we visited the communal collective settlement of Ein Yahav (the building of settlements in the Aravah had only just begun). We were all stunned by the beauty of the desert landscape. Moshe Shamir made the comment: "The further south we go, the more silent we are." And Yani Avidov expressed the same thought in his own way: "We are a small nation, but we have a vast desert." At Ein Yahav we were greeted by Shai Ben-Eliyahu, the secretary of the moshav and the initiator of the settlement in this region. Shai took us on a guided tour, pointing out items of interest and giving us a lecture on the history of the locality and the development of the farm. When he had finished, Nathan was invited "to say a few words." All eyes were on him and he was clearly embarrassed. He said: "Shai, what marvelous Hebrew you speak. . . ." But the members insisted on a speech, and he agreed to oblige them:

> The problem of the youth of today is that it suffers from "a sense of guilt." Some of its negative actions are a compensation for this sense of guilt, which arises from a feeling of inadequacy and the lack of a means of self-expression. The difference between the young people of Ayin Yahav and

young people elsewhere in the world is that here they are free from a sense of guilt; they are doing something great and original of their own. *In genesis there is no guilt. . . .*

On a visit to the Suez Canal zone we met and talked with soldiers and officers; these were men with whom Nathan enjoyed a strong sense of rapport, and he was in high spirits. He glanced at the Canal and remarked: "The Suez Canal . . . once it was the 'Dizengoff Street' of the British Empire, the greatest empire in the world. They did us a favor, and gave us the Balfour Declaration as an act of kindness. Since then, in less than fifty years, everything has changed. Look at what is left of the British Empire—a few economic headaches and a lot of strikes. And who sits now on the banks of the Canal, in their 'Dizengoff'? The sons of daydreamers, the descendants of the men who accepted the Declaration—Rothschild, Sokolov, Weizmann. There are empires that have fallen into decline, and there are heritages that shall stand for ever."

Travel was his workshop, a mobile studio into which he brought paints, compounds, brushes, designs, frames and daylight. During every one of his journeys Nathan made copious notes (I understand that only a few of these have survived, since Alterman was by nature averse to leaving behind rough drafts and sketches), and some time later these would appear in print, in the form of a poem, a song or an article. All of these publications are remarkable for the wealth of detail contained in them.

When we visited a military industries factory, Nathan was chiefly interested in two points: the geographical origins of the workers, and the development of parachute flares. This was a period of mass immigration to Israel, and it seems that Nathan's attention was focused on the revolutionary transition that had taken place—from a nation of unarmed exiles, to a people in its own land, forging its own armaments. In a poem that he published shortly afterward, he wrote:

> And when I saw the African Jew bending over
>   the furnace,
> To draw out the ingot of red-hot steel,
> And passing it with his tongs to the immigrant
>   from the Balkans,
> I saw a people standing firm on its foundations.

The places of origin of the workers were also carefully recorded:

> They are Jews from Tripoli, Turkey, San'a and
>   Luvov,
> From Sofia and Yassi, clean-shaven, heavy-
>   bearded.

The parachute flare was something that interested Nathan immensely. He was told that the factory had succeeded in producing shells and rockets, machine guns and mortars, but with the manufacturing of the flare there were a number of problems: it was difficult to devise an instrument of such enormous light-intensity—hundreds of thousands of candlepower—required to light up the battlefield for a space of several minutes, allowing for the identification of danger points, observation of the enemy's dispositions and choice of targets. Nathan noted down all these points. An echo of this preoccupation is to be found in his poem *Ben-Gurion on the Verge of Taking a Step*:

> And as if with sudden light, light of dire
> emergency,
> With light of perception,
> All the landscape shall be illumined.

On the eve of the Suez Operation a consignment of arms was brought to Israel from France, in vessels of the French Navy. The whole business was kept a close secret, but I thought it appropriate to invite Nathan to watch the unloading of the arms in the Haifa port at dead of night. This night visit was the inspiration for another poem which David Ben-Gurion recited from the podium of the Knesset on October 15, 1956; it was from this poem that the public first became aware of the drastic improvement in our situation.

> I dreamed last night of steel, much steel, new
> steel.
> The bearer of laden canisters, ringing on iron
> chains,
> Arrives from afar, sets foot on the shore and as
> imagination turns into reality,

With the first touch of the land he becomes the
expression of the power of the Jews.

Nathan had not known that David Ben-Gurion
was going to read his poem to the Knesset, and suddenly he found himself in the center of a national
sensation, bombarded with praise and gratitude
from every quarter. "People in the street shake my
hand and thank me for this," he wrote in a letter to
Nehemiah Argov. This letter also testified to a great
depth of emotion: "And yet I would like it to be
made known to him, to David Ben-Gurion, in the
most positive terms, how moved I am by the great
and unexpected honor that I have received. To hear
the whole of my poem from the lips of the highest
and most eminent man in the land, and on the most
prestigious of all stages (compelling the entire Knesset to hear the poem from beginning to end!) and to
receive such eloquent and sincere praise from the
highest quarters—has any writer in our times been
more generously rewarded?"

Nathan's travels around the country were not
aimed solely at first-hand acquisition of facts. He
also wanted to study the growth of our national
spirit, to feel the strength planted in its soil and
manufactured in its enterprises.

In the early sixties Nathan joined us in a visit
to the Atomic Research complex near Dimona. His
interest in this new phase in the nation's development was enormous, but at the same time his feel-
ings were divided. After the visit he sent me a letter,
which included the following remarks:

> Allow me to thank you . . . for letting me share the secret of something which those responsible for it and aware of it must regard both as a mighty source of salvation, and it is bound to influence the whole of our system of values regarding day-to-day problems.

The relationship between Ben-Gurion and Alterman was of a very special nature. Ben-Gurion saw Alterman as a sensitive judge, with a close awareness of the experiences and aspirations of the Jewish people, motivated by a conscience that never faltered and equipped with "one of the most lyrical instruments of the Jewish renaissance—when he exonerates it is a great privilege; when he condemns he commands a reexamination of one's thoughts and deeds."

Alterman's respect for Ben-Gurion was firm and enduring; it never wavered for a moment. For him, Ben-Gurion was a part of the landscape of Eretz Israel, the landscape of his people and his country. More than once he disagreed with him, but he never hesitated to express in public his sincere and wholehearted admiration for the great man.

Nathan openly opposed Ben-Gurion's policy on a number of points. On the disbandment of the Palmach he wrote: "A great miracle and jewel, a wonder to all men / Has been wrapped up and sent back into history!" On the issue of "reparations" from Germany he exclaimed: "Are we to stop our insistence / With bold and firm voice / On the justice of our demands / In return for blood-money?" He disagreed with Ben-Gurion's policy of military government, and toward the end of his life he opposed him most fiercely on the question of "Greater Israel." After the Six Day War he could not accept the view that Israel should withdraw from the occupied territories "in exchange for a true peace." But for as long as he lived he supported Ben-Gurion's views on statehood and Zionism. Like him he rejected Zionism without immigration and like him he rejected Stalinism and Stalinists: "We should indeed envy this ability to race on / For twenty-five years without friction and flaw / With eyes tightly closed—to the light / And lips tightly sealed—to the truth." And like Ben-Gurion he was disgusted by the parochial approach that characterized political life in Israel.

His close identification with Ben-Gurion was most clearly in evidence at the time of the "Lavon Affair." It was in fact Nathan who first exposed the scandal, through his weekly column in the newspaper *Davar*, shaking the people and the leadership, and subsequently he waged a tenacious and courageous campaign against what he called "the distortion of justice," and supported "the Old Man" in all his actions, especially his resignation from Mapai and the establishment of Rafi.

Alterman was the living conscience of this new movement. We never took a decision on any serious matter without first consulting him.

Nathan made his views known in poetry, in prose and in newspaper articles. It was also in this period that he published his most ironical work, *The Last Mask;* in the dialogue between "Hedgehog," the veteran campaigner, and "Bonte," the new immigrant, he ruthlessly satirized the institutions of government. "The time for an inquiry has long since arrived, an inquiry which will tear down conventions and reform its antiquated foundations," was Nathan's message. The inquiry which ensued was indeed acrimonious:

> Once, between two votes,
> A curious man asked:
> What could equal the greatness of the
>   problems?
> I answered: the pettiness of the small-minded
>   bureaucrat.

There is a reference in the book to the conflict between the leadership and David Ben-Gurion:

> If this hierarchy had been working alone,
> We would now be beyond all help. . . .
> But the Creator has rescued His people from its
>   clutches
> By the hand of a man whose name is
>   forgotten. . . .

It was useless trying to ignore David Ben-Gurion: "Even if we wipe away his footprints from the annals of history, history itself will become his footprint." Alterman ridiculed the idea that investigation of the "Lavon Affair" would open up a fearful "Pandora's box" containing "gigantic ghosts and storms and stone-shattering tempests"; he commented that all these things were nothing compared with what was really in the box, whose contents were bound to have truly devastating effects:

> Within me there dwell—the box said
> In a hushed whisper—
> The morbid fears
> And the bitter dread
> Of that stunted body
> Which is called the Secretariat.

If the "Affair" brought Nathan to his highest pitch of vociferous protest—against injustice, apathy, dogma and small-mindedness—in the question of the unity of the land, Nathan felt his highest sense of obligation, of love for the land, its scenery and its history.

After the Six Day War we spent a great deal of time touring the new frontiers. We visited the medicinal springs near Tubas on the banks of the Jordan River, the Golan Heights ("Oh, Og king of Bashan," he joked, "see what has become of you now!"), and the Gaza Strip. Here Nathan walked among the palms and fig trees like a man entranced. In the ancient synagogue to the south of Gaza, he was much impressed when he found that the original stone floor had survived: "You can destroy a Philistine tower," he said, "but an Israelite floor stays!" We visited the refugee camps, to inspect the work of reconstruction that was being undertaken there. Nathan coined a phrase when he spoke of "the Third Israel"—an Israel responsible for the rehabilitation of the Arab refugees, whose lot was a great deal worse than that of "the First" and "the Second" Israel.

With Rehavam Ze'evi, who was then Commanding General of the Central District, we toured Wadi Kelt. Leading the party, as we climbed the twisting paths of the wadi, were Aryeh Regev and Gad Manella, later to fall victim to an ambush by Arab snipers in this very place.

When I went to invite him to accompany us in this tour I saw that Nathan was ill and suffering great pain. I tried to persuade him not to join us on this occasion and I promised that we would arrange another tour for a later date. At the time I thought that I had persuaded him, but on the eve of the tour he came to my house and declared quite categorically that he intended to travel with us. The next day he arrived punctually at the rendezvous.

Nathan's face was always rather pale, but on this occasion his pallor was perceptibly and ominously worse. All day he touched no food. He climbed with us up all the narrow paths, and I could tell that it was not the muscles that were moving his feet, but the willpower of a man determined, whatever the cost to his health, to study the landscape of the land that he loved. "I must not miss the smells of Jericho," he said with a forced smile, as he put the steel helmet on his head. In the jeep that drove up to the wadi he was as jovial as a man in the best of health, without a care and happy with his lot. He defined his illness as: "A temporary disturbance of the brain caused by an obscure and passing malfunction of the digestive system."

On a Sabbath afternoon—his last Sabbath before becoming bedridden—he came to my house, "in order to conclude the travels that we have made." My wife Sonya offered him a cup of tea, but he declined. I remember vividly, almost word for word, what he then said:

"We have seen the country. There is an empty entity about it that awaits our labors. This is *our* entity, the Jewish entity from the cradle of history, and not the recently invented Palestinian entity. If there really is a dispute here between two peoples, between a Palestinian people supposedly uprooted from their land and a Jewish people that supposedly uprooted them—then we have been wrong all along.

"This is not a problem of explaining our position to the world, it is a fundamental problem. And a fundamental debate is not to be avoided, for it shall determine whether we win or lose. Of course there is a conflict here between two nations, the Jewish nation and the Arab nation, between a nation that is in a minority in every country in the world (except Israel) and a nation that is in a majority in eighteen states in the Middle East. And although there are many minorities in their states, the majority status of the Arabs is never called into question. Our dispute with the Palestinians is not over a name, but over a country; it is not a dispute over equal rights, but over our right to live as a majority in one place in the world."

And he concluded his speech with a declaration that still rings in my ears: "Our security problems are the security problems of a *state* and the security problems of a *people.*"

His love of the land was absolute. He enlisted the support of poets, writers and friends in his vision of the integrity of the whole of Eretz Israel. He brought together wide and disparate bodies of opinion, men of all parties, of all ages. This vision accompanied him to the end. Only once did I ever hear him express real pessimism: "In this struggle we cannot hope to stand up to both the Russians and the Americans."

If you want to learn what a country really is, you should not only study its dimensions, but also its qualities—the spirit of the people, its history, its poetry, its legends, its fears and hopes. The inner landscape determines the real identity of a country no less effectively than the outer landscape and it is this that gives meaning to nation and to people.

Could there be an Israel without Alterman's poetry? Sometimes his poetry is like dew on a flower, sometimes it is the people's morale, working like the pulse of reality, it is like the first smile of a newborn baby, it is like "the wing of a creative spirit . . . stamping on summits shrouded in mists, a lawgiver and a prophet.'' Sometimes it is a song heard from the radio, sometimes it rings in our ears as the background music to actions and events. Sometimes it is a solemn and mysterious poem, sometimes it is the rhythm of an army on the march, and sometimes the prayers of a people.

> It is the war of the people whose shepherd you
>   are,
> It is the war of the lips of the fighting man,
> It is the war of the people whose teacher you
>   are,
> Teaching the wisdom of the ancients, in curse
>   and in vow.

Nathan loved Israel, the people, the land and the spirit. He loved it with a Jewish love, with skepticism, with extremes of conflicting emotion, with humility, with jealousy, with perception and wit, with sorrow, with regret and pride. He loved it with devotion and pain. He filled it with sounds and rhythms of unprecedented originality and sweetness. And everything that he was, and everything that he wrote, turned into music, with soft cadences and deafening crescendos, *Eroica* and Funeral March, lullaby and wedding song, melodies of legend and songs of day-to-day life.

His voice echoes, and the echoes of distant voices respond. He sang of the land of Israel, working, fighting, beautiful and whole. And the Israel that he left behind him was a nation singing.

ERNST DAVID BERGMANN
Creating a Future Out of Naught

> *I am convinced that the State of Israel needs a defense research program of its own, so that we shall never again be as lambs led to the slaughter.*
>
> E. D. BERGMANN

WHEN PROFESSOR CHAIM WEIZMANN was contemplating the foundation of a scientific institute (the Daniel Sieff Institute) in Rehovot, he approached Professor Albert Einstein and asked him to recommend one of his best students for the post of director of the institute. Einstein nominated an outstanding young scientist, then in his thirties—Ernst David

Bergmann, scion of an eminent German rabbinical family. Weizmann was deeply impressed, not only by the man's exceptional scientific aptitude but also by his broad political awareness, and for a long time he cherished the idea that Professor Bergmann would one day fulfill a role of the highest importance in the leadership of the state: he saw him as a future candidate for the presidency.

With the foundation of the state and the increasing importance of the issue of defense, as it became necessary to concentrate the best brains of the country in the Ministry of Defense, Professor Bergmann was given the post of Head of the Scientific Department of the Ministry. Later he was also appointed Scientific Adviser to the Minister of Defense and Chairman of the Atomic Energy Commission in the Prime Minister's Office.

Professor Bergmann was a man of passionate scientific vision. Bergmann's scientific vision was attracted to Ben-Gurion's statesmanlike vision—and the plowman met the sower. From the start a firm rapport, both scientific and personal, was forged between them, and this collaboration was to make a powerful contribution to the state.

Ernst Bergmann was of medium height. His pale face was delicate and refined, and he used a number of different pairs of glasses for reading and writing. He used to work about eighteen hours a day, in organization, in administration, and in the pursuit of his own research. He was one of the most energetic men I ever met in my life. He never relaxed and he was never tired.

He was an astonishing polymath. His abilities bordered on genius—a phenomenal memory, a rare capacity for learning and teaching, an outstanding analytical talent and a series of wide-ranging scientific achievements. He was able both to rationalize ideas and to create ideas.

He educated a generation of Israeli scientists. He was to the Israeli science community what Berl was to the Israeli labor community. As a teacher he had a sharp eye for the qualities of his students, capable of freeing them from personal diffidence, and inspiring them with original hope, endowing them with intellectual vision, and subsequently accompanying them along the way, with patient encouragement and tireless guidance, until they reached their highest level of self-expression, the discovery of their full potential, the summit of their ability.

As an intellectual he was an absolute positivist. He abhorred all that was negative. Denials made no impression on him. He ignored inadequacy and despised shortsightedness. He had the ability to say "yes" at times when "no" and "impossible" were habitually heard.

As a man he was made of sensitive and refined material, a sort of human silk. He loved people, and he enjoyed their society. His personal courtesy and his universal curiosity made him the central figure in any company. His presence radiated an atmosphere of gentility, depth and perception.

His suggestions were not always realistic, but frequently suggestions of his that seemed unrealistic were transformed into facts that changed the face of reality.

His personality involved a great many contradictions: by nature he was an open man, but the context of his work in the Ministry of Defense obliged him to be secretive. He was agreeable in his contacts with people, but his status aroused jealousy and opposition. And although he tended to answer "yes" to every proposition put to him, a habit sometimes regarded with suspicion, he held consistent and unshakable opinions. He described this himself in one of his letters to me: "Every man of science who works in the field of defense, must *surrender* an important part of the researcher's life—that is, contact with his colleagues, both personally and through publications in the international press—and he is obliged to come to terms with a considerable degree of anonymity."

Because he was both a positivist and an optimist, he invited upon himself the criticism of many of his colleagues in the scientific world. They claimed that he was advocating things that were not at all practicable, and sometimes they even accused him of improvisation. His close personal relationship with David Ben-Gurion only aggravated the jealousy of others, and deepened his isolation within the milieu to which he belonged.

He was not always viewed with favor by administrative officials. And especially, naturally enough, when it was a question of finance. He insisted that they did not understand the issues involved. "There *are* things more important than money, unfortunately *they too* cost money," Bergmann used to say sarcastically.

And although he was well liked by most of the people with whom he came into contact, he did not always gain satisfaction in his dealings with defense experts. Naturally, strategy begins close to the ground ("Politics is geography," Napoleon once said), it is not an inspirational gift concerned with abstract scientific possibilities, dependent on processes that have yet to be proved; theories are of little value in comparison with the real weapons of war. For it is not enough to invent things, they must be meticulously tested, they must stand up under combat conditions and prove their worth as operational equipment. Bergmann represented the future. and on behalf of the future he demanded efforts beyond the scope of the present, although even the demands of the present were never fully realized.

Things sometimes reached the level of large-scale confrontation. A high-ranking army officer once demanded that I transfer Ernst Bergmann to a different post. In the letter that I sent to this officer I tried to explain to him the injustice of his demand: "Dr. Bergmann has substantial rights—rights which in my view have been conferred not only on account of his years of service, but also on account of his record of *achievements,* by which I mean that he has recommended and carried through courses of action that have proved their worth and that he has done this *single-handed,* and against the advice of others. I believe that much of the opposition to him arises from the fact that in many cases he has been right, *and the only one who has been right.*"

Some of his ideas were implemented, some were left as visions for the future. Both categories have a powerful vitality which deserves examination.

I worked with Ernst Bergmann for about thirteen years (1952–65), and I did not know whether to be pleased or sorry when he decided to accompany us into the political wilderness (with the formation of Rafi). The pleasure needs no explanation! The sorrow was over the vacuum that would be created within the defense establishment. For much of my time I had acted as a kind of middleman between David Ben-Gurion, as Prime Minister and Minister of Defense, and Ernst Bergmann, his scientific adviser. In this post I was mainly responsible for the practical application of things and the working out of priorities. It was a broad responsibility, not always circumscribed, but its objective was clear: to advance the scientific progress of Israel to the furthest possible extent. In this I was greatly helped by Moniah Mardor, Director of the Strategic Weapons Development Authority.

At the beginning of the 1950s, the whole world, including Israel, was much excited at the mighty potential created by the new atomic capability, for peaceful purposes. Being a country of meager water resources and also a country lacking independent oil reserves, the atomic potential had a particular appeal for us: it would enable us both to desalinate seawater and to generate electricity. Together with Ernst Bergmann we had to take the first steps in this unfamiliar sphere, where both the prospects and the dangers were an unknown quantity.

The extent of naïveté inherent in our approach in those days may be illustrated by two letters sent by David Ben-Gurion to Ernst Bergmann. The letter sent from Sdeh Boker (November 18, 1954) includes the following:

> Now that Abba Eban has made our atomic researches public in the forum of the United Nations—I shall tell you an anecdote: about two weeks ago I was visited by Dr. Markowitz, the conductor; his wife and a friend were also in the party. After we had talked for a while, Markowitz suddenly said that he wished to tell me a secret, and he asked the other two to leave the room. When we were left alone he told me that a few weeks ago he had a dream; in his dream he was sitting with me in Sdeh Boker and asking me why we were not engaged in atomic research. When he woke up he went on thinking about this and he came to the conclusion that nothing would exalt our prestige in the world more than atomic research. I told him that we had already been working on this for several years.

"Exalt our prestige in the world"—how do you do that? Why is it necessary? In a letter to Bergmann a month later, December 12, Ben-Gurion wrote:

I have been bathing here in the hot springs of Tiberias. The manager of the establishment tells me that as long ago as 1912 a scientist found radioactive deposits here, but the level of radioactivity was measured and found to be weak (it was measured then on the "Mach units" scale, and the number of units was small). . . . The manager also tells me that local doctors are worried about the level of radioactivity and fear that it may lead to sterility among farm animals and among people as well. . . .

In any event, we needed to translate abstract desire into the language of action. Even in this area two world views came into conflict, the "realistic" and the "visionary." The advocates of the "realistic" approach insisted that first of all, as a matter of principle, it was necessary to establish what was needed for the state, needed in a practical sense, and which demands should be accorded first priority, and which second. Atomic energy, they said, was nothing more than an idea, and perhaps a hope, but one set in the distant future, while in the present more urgent needs abounded, and were still to be satisfied. "We do not have the money to buy wheat, or even rice; are we to squander our resources on a tenuous technological dream?" asked one member of the Knesset. And secondly, it was claimed that it was not within the scientific, administrative or financial capacity of Israel to enter a field reserved for the greatest of the world's nations. "The great powers will never forgive us if we try to embark on a program that is beyond our capability as a small people," was a claim often heard in the Knesset. And the Treasury Minister said: "In Israel we are rationing eggs to one a week—and these people want atomic energy. . . ."

The advocates of the "visionary" approach were less articulate; their position was that we were obliged to pursue not only Israel's current requirements but also to explore the possibilities—scientific and technological—that the world was opening up before our generation and the generations of the future, and that the starting point should not be present needs but future potential. We must attempt to harness this potential, in its earliest stages, even in areas with which we were unfamiliar, so that we might be among the progressive, not the backward, nations of our times. As for priorities, these could not be determined only on the basis of the pressures of the past. Our future should also be taken into account in our national priorities.

Naturally the debate on principles also involved the parallel schools of scientific thought, and a vigorous polemic was waged between them. In a letter to me (January 1, 1957), one of the most distinguished scientists in the country expressed accurately and elegantly an opinion widespread among Israel's scientific community: "In this country we have achieved great and sensational things in all areas where *spiritual forces* have been a decisive factor: we have built 'Burma Roads,' we have grown tomatoes in saline soil, we have brought in hundreds of thousands of new immigrants and found a creative role for them and so on, but we have made no significant scientific and technological advances and we are not likely to do so *since no spiritual force can compel a screw to fit the wrong kind of nut."* And the letter ends with the remark: "In our present circumstances it is not within our power to carry this out."

The majority of scientists believed it to be their conscientious duty not only to enable Israel to benefit from the developments made possible by scientific advance, but also to prevent her from becoming involved in futile and unproductive adventures, such as would lead to a waste of effort on the part of researchers, loss of research time and excessive expenditure of public funds.

Against them, in the scientific world, Professor Ernst Bergmann stood almost alone. His theories seemed slightly ambivalent, and his pragmatic suggestions very conjectural. He put forward examples from Sweden and Norway—"where they even use atomic power for cutting down trees." He claimed that the installation of atomic plant would be the best way of developing the Negev: "The conquest of the Negev," he wrote, "requires that the Israeli intelligentsia be transplanted to the Negev. As long as the research establishments and personnel of the state are concentrated in the north, there can be no hope of turning the Negev into a viable part of the country."

He claimed that within a decade we would be able to produce electricity from an atomic reactor, also to desalinate sea water: "We have sufficient water to provide for the northern half of the country; if we also wish to irrigate the southern half for purposes of settlement, we must double our current water resources, that means an extra 1.5 billion cubic meters per year. This can be achieved only by desalination, and desalination can be effected by using the steam from an atomic reactor. This is a massive undertaking, but it can be implemented within twenty years."

In July 1956 he presented me with a lengthy memorandum including a variety of options: we could purchase a reactor from America, Canada, or France, or even build it ourselves. That same memorandum included the two following clauses:

> *The Small Reactor.* If the small reactor cannot be established at Rehovot, it will be best to build it close to the sea, for example at Nebi Rubin.
> *The Large Reactor.* Its logical site is the Negev, as the nucleus of a scientific community. An alternative site would be Nebi Rubin.

And he concluded the memorandum with the following sentence: "If we pursue all these paths, we may be confident that some of them at least will lead us to our goal."

Bergmann did not realize how accurate his prediction was. Eight years after this memorandum was written, a "small" atomic reactor was operating at Nebi Rubin, a large reactor at Dimona.

When we embarked on the installation of the reactor at Nebi Rubin and later the reactor at Dimona, we had no idea of the difficulties that were to confront us on the way. We had no money (we were forced to launch a fund-raising appeal of our own) and no technicians; we recruited graduates from the Technion and turned them into nuclear technicians. The level of foreign aid fluctuated, and we were forced to adapt to sudden changes. We were subject to vociferous criticism both at home and abroad. It is possible that if we had foreseen all the difficulties on the way, we might have decided that the odds were against us. But a vision, like love, depends on a certain measure of blindness, blindness which turned out, in the final analysis, to be something perfectly rational.

The reactors gave Israel a new impetus, they "exalted" our prestige in the words of Dr. Markowitz's dream. The project also gave a tremendous boost to the development of the Negev, to the expansion and development of Beersheba and Dimona. It also made a sizable contribution to the establishment of the Ben-Gurion University in Beersheba. This last item was also something that Bergmann had foreseen. "If the population of the state rises to three million in the course of the second decade it will be necessary to build another university . . . the best site for such a university is the Negev," Ernst Bergmann wrote in August 1958.

When David Ben-Gurion asked me in October

1957 to review the progress of the atomic program, I wrote in my report: "There is indeed a group of colleagues working on the project, but these colleagues do not constitute a team. . . . Dr. Bergmann is the most eminent member of this group as regards public relations and he is also the man who believed in the feasibility of developing this field before such belief was fashionable. More than that, he is totally committed to the project and I know of no man capable of taking his place as chairman of the Atomic Energy Commission."

Bergmann was much concerned by the kind of pragmatism that sometimes leads to inertia, something with which many of our best people were infected. "There are those who say," he wrote, "that it is possible to purchase everything that we need, including knowledge and experience, from abroad. This attitude worries me." And he added: "I am convinced . . . that the State of Israel needs a defense research program of its own, so that we shall never again be as lambs led to the slaughter."

For all the many years that we worked together he never wavered in his insistence that Israel must, and could, achieve independence in the four vital areas of existence: energy, water, food and armaments.

Energy, he claimed, could be created from anything, from solar power, from atomic reactors, from bituminous rock, from wave-power, from the wind. Energy was the Achilles' heel of the state. And if we pursued a broad-based policy, we would enjoy the fruits of independence.

Water could be obtained through the desalination of sea water, through the purification of waste water, and through the artificial stimulation of rainfall. By these means we would be relieved of the hazards of drought and chronic water shortage and be capable of becoming a fertile and independent country. . . .

"A nation that has water," he said, "will also have more arable land. And a nation with trees, gardens and fields will increase its agricultural potential and also achieve an improvement in climate, with long summers giving way to prolonged springs."

Food could be obtained from the land and the sea. We had the potential to develop new varieties of agricultural products, to grow plants in the desert and to make advances in oceanographic research. "A nation self-sufficient in food will find its independence secure."

As for armaments, Bergmann claimed that Israel was capable of meeting almost all her own needs, and of developing within the country technological assets preferable to anything that could be imported from abroad, assets that would give the State a formidable international standing and independence on the battlefield. Independence that would not be just a new declaration, but a new reality.

Bergmann believed very strongly in our ability to achieve this end. In general, he believed that the Jews of the Diaspora had been saved from the backwardness that affected other peoples "thanks to the study of the Torah." This had preserved their "rational capacity," an asset which continued to exist in contemporary Israel. Bergmann believed that the world is full of latent treasures—chemical, physical and biological—and it is only the habitual laziness of mankind that prevents him from drawing them out, identifying them and exploiting them in a concentrated effort aimed at the enrichment of life and at greater freedom for individuals and nations, even the smallest nations.

The success of a man's ideas and projects does not invariably guarantee the man's personal success. Ideas which have turned into projects gather new people around them and lead to the creation of new administrative processes and, needless to say, new rivalries and sensitivities. This also happened to some extent in the case of Professor Bergmann.

The range of the research continued to expand, sometimes outstripping our capacity to cope with it. The new manufacturing concerns that we had established or promoted—the aircraft industry, the military and electronic industries, the optical industry—were also beginning to show a growing interest in research and development. It was hard for Professor Bergmann—and not only for him—to coordinate and control the ever-expanding research program. He had the feeling that with the expansion of the program, his own role was somewhat diminished.

When David Ben-Gurion resigned from the Government and Levi Eshkol was appointed in his place, Professor Bergmann embarked on a new campaign aimed at the broadening of scientific research, not only in the field of defense but in the wider interests of the State as a whole. He expressed these demands both to Eshkol and to me. Eshkol suggested to him that he put his ideas into writing and present a comprehensive research scheme, a kind of master plan for the State.

Bergmann wrote a memorandum and presented it to Eshkol on December 22, 1964. This plan has lost none of its vitality and imagination even today, some fifteen years later, and it is virtually certain that its relevance will continue to be recognized for many more years to come.

In the preface to the memorandum Professor Bergmann claimed that a modern State is capable of choosing between two approaches, of which one says that a country must "contribute to the advancement of world knowledge" and the other says that research should be based "on the requirements of the State—both short and long term." In his view, there was a negative attitude in Israel toward the first approach, and no clear attitude toward the second.

There was a widespread view that "it is possible to buy the knowledge that we require and therefore there is no need to invest money and effort in independent research, even research for a specific purpose." Professor Bergmann rejected this attitude, claiming that if there are no experts trained in a certain field there is no authority qualified to decide what should be bought, and how to exploit the purchased knowledge. Furthermore, a state which sells knowledge is not likely to sell *new knowledge,* that it has not yet exploited itself, and such a state would keep this technical advantage to itself. The only knowledge that it would be prepared to sell us— would be *obsolete knowledge,* of no value. Also, knowledge amassed in one country is not always suited to the conditions of another.

All research, even "pure" research, is capable of leading to results of practical value, said Bergmann. "The prestige of a country depends to no small extent on its efforts in the sphere of research, especially pure research, and there can be no higher education without a considerable degree of research. Research," commented Bergmann with a measure of sarcasm, "is a costly commodity, *and especially in areas which have a close bearing on the problems of the future.*"

And then came the plan itself, referring in detail to the areas of science and the economy:

Mechanics—"Metallurgy in Israel is not sufficiently developed," Professor Bergmann believed, "even in the academic institutions. The exploitation of rare and precious metals and their alloys demands research into their mechanical and electrical properties. This also applies to ceramic materials capable of standing up to high temperatures." In his view there was also a case for "developing systems of *examination without destruction,* so that it may be possible to examine products or components without the need to destroy them or melt them down."

Physics—He saw two areas requiring special

emphasis. One of these was the development of lasers, which would bring about a revolution no less significant than that caused by transistors in the areas of communications, optics and electronics; the other was "a system of magnifying a very weak light on the field of vision at night—the magnification of starlight. The difference between day and night is relative—and relativities can be changed."

Electronics—Microelectronics must be developed. This involves the miniaturization of instruments and components, as a means of reducing the weight and volume of products and increasing their adaptability. And parallel to this, the development of computers. "In another ten years," he predicted, "our entire commercial and social life will be conducted with the aid of computers, and we must be in a position to master their logic and devise building systems economical in money and materials."

Agriculture—"Israel," he explained, "is faced with three fundamental problems: agricultural development of the desert; the war against pests; the exploitation of agricultural production as a basis for industry. As regards arid zone agriculture, the problem is the correct exploitation of water resources and the introduction of new plant varieties suited to a desert climate." In his opinion, we needed to "investigate the properties which enable the plants of the desert to retain their moisture and resist evaporation while preserving their ability to [with]stand salinity." He also believed that it was possible to limit evaporation further by artificial means—"such as spraying the plants with plastic coating, which will permit them to breathe but prevent evaporation."

Professor Bergmann also proposed the introduction of desert crops, something capable of bringing enormous advantage to the nation's economy: reducing the size of the desert and boosting the country's harvests.

The problem of the fight against pests was raised by Professor Bergmann to a new level of importance. "The war against pests is one of the central problems of humanity: it also involves the problem of fighting disease-carrying insects, especially in a climate where the damage caused by insects is rapid and effective. It is said," Bergmann continued, "that the problem of Africa is an insect problem, and one insect in particular—the tsetse fly, which ruins vast quantities of produce." (Israeli scientists helped in African projects to fight this insect and is able today to offer assistance to other nations in which the pest is endemic.) He maintained that the classic approach—developing new and more toxic chemical pesticides—is not effective since it builds up resistance to the chemicals. He believed that better prospects were offered by new methods, "such as the *sterilization* of insects by radiation or chemical processes, or the infecting of insects with parasites."

The third fundamental problem facing agriculture in Israel was the exploitation of its products as raw materials for industry. Just as cotton is a manufacturing element, so could other crops, medicinal herbs, for example, provide materials for an expanding pharmaceutical industry. Agriculture is designed primarily for the production of food. "But the food market is not flexible, it is possible to stabilize it— if we can find new uses for produce, by-products, surpluses and waste." (For example, the use made of orange peel could be extended to the peels of all fruits.)

Similarly, when oil reserves dwindle it would be necessary to find "substitutes for oil as a fuel, and as a base for the petrochemical industry. The place of oil as a fuel could be taken by atomic energy; for the petrochemical industry the best substitute would be found in agricultural products containing sugar, starch or cellulose. It is to be anticipated that in the future agriculture will assume a position of central importance in the world economy, and we shall be compelled to think of agriculture in the same terms as industry, that is, we shall be concerned with the propagation of plants suitable for fermentation processes to a degree beyond the conventional range of the agriculture planning today."

Mines—We must not be content with "the improvement of the relatively poor mines that exist in Israel today (those producing phosphates, copper and iron); taking a broader perspective, we must ensure that ships arriving in Eilat will not be empty but will carry a useful cargo—such as raw materials from Asia and Africa, and these should be processed in refineries set up in the vicinity of Eilat with a view to reexport."

He believed that better use could be made of the raw materials that we possess in great quantities:

bromine, magnesium, phosphates and fluorine. Magnesium could be a basic ingredient for many processes, since it is a light metal which can also be cheap, and the magnesium deposits in the Dead Sea are enormous. Phosphate could be a basic ingredient not only for chemical fertilizers, but also for the manufacture of plastics and fire-resistant products. And of course—the enormous potential involved in sea water desalination was not to be ignored.

He believed firmly in the feasibility of amassing vast quantities of mineral extractions during the desalination process. These could also be exploited. "The British, for example, have devised a method of obtaining uranium from sea water. And they say that it is only three times more expensive."

Professor Bergmann then turned his attention to the type of industry "which manufactures products the value of which is determined not by the *raw materials,* but by the *inventive energy* invested in them. Such industry could be divided into four main areas: plastics, delicate chemicals, medicinal products, electronics. There is virtually no limit on the development of the plastics industry in the future. The invention of new varieties of plastic material, with new properties, and the use of existing materials for new processes—all this calls for and justifies research and development work."

The chemical materials required in the world today fall into two categories: those needed in quantities of thousands of tons, and those needed in quantities of a few kilograms. The second type are rare chemicals which are especially useful for certain kinds of laboratory research. The demand for them is great, and the supply limited, because their preparation requires a level of manpower that is neither available, nor cheap, in most countries. "This is an area of development suitable for Israel."

Contrary to general belief, the electronics industry could also be developed in Israel, "so long as it is based on original research and high standards of manufacture."

Within a space of a few years, reality was to prove that in this respect too, Bergmann's vision was eminently realistic.

At this point Bergmann made detailed recommendations regarding new areas of research or the further development of current research. He believed that Israel was capable of producing uranium "from the sea or from phosphates." This would give us independence in the future, when the need to be supplied by atomic energy became more pressing. Atomic radiation could be put to a variety of uses: as a means of producing new properties in existing plants, new varieties of organism and fungi for antibiotics; it could also be used as a preservative for food, both for home consumption and export, and as a medium for the improvement of the physical properties of plastic materials, of wood, and metal, including electricity.

It was also necessary to explore new and supplementary fields. Israel must obtain silicotrones (instruments for the acceleration of atomic molecules to high energy levels) as a means of broadening the research potential involved in reactors, "to open up new horizons for physicists."

Special attention should be given to certain aspects of space research—for meteorological purposes in particular. "Knowledge of the upper stratosphere is essential for both civilian and military aviation; for the forecasting of weather; for the artificial stimulation of rainfall."

Oceanographic research was required for the purpose of expanding food supplies, the emphasis being on the development of fisheries and submarine agriculture, as well as on the physical investigation of the seashore and the properties of the sea.

At the end of his outline plan, Professor Bergmann again stressed that "the time has come to study, from a chemical and biological standpoint, the human brain, its normal and pathological processes, and the possibilities of increasing its efficiency—memory improvement, for example," something which in his opinion "is a relatively straightforward chemical problem."

"In general," he said, "I see a need to turn human beings into an object of research. Population planning, for example, requires the study of human genetics, the influence of genetic and environmental factors on child development, the influence of national origins and their absorption in our society in the future.

"Human engineering is required as a means of exploiting the mechanical and intellectual capabilities of people, so that we may design tools and in-

struments suited to the abilities of their operators.
... A nation poor in manpower must attach great
importance to this issue."

Some fifteen years have passed since these
words were written or spoken. But the words have
not lost their flavor and when we look at the
thoughts that he expressed in the past, we rediscover
the shape of our future.

It is also interesting to note the reactions of Eshkol (then Prime Minister) and of David Ben-Gurion
(then a private citizen in Sdeh Boker) to Bergmann's
proposals.

Eshkol tried to persuade Professor Bergmann to
come down from his Olympian heights and offer a
more practical scheme: "What we need now," said
Eshkol, "is that you should try to give a simple,
realistic, practical and financial estimate of what
this will mean to us over the next ten years."

By contrast, David Ben-Gurion wrote him the
following letter (dated December 30, 1964):

> I have read your plan for a scientific
> research program with great interest. Two
> sections in particular aroused my curiosity:
> 1. Psychopharmacological products ca-
> pable of favorably influencing the intellec-
> tual and spiritual processes of the human
> being. Are there really such products? Who
> has experimented with them, and with
> what results? Are they available in this
> country?
> 2. The study of the brain. Is there any-
> body in Israel currently studying this won-

derful organ? In my opinion this is the most useful research of all (although I am also in favor of pure research which does not lead to measurable advantage) for there is no instrument more precious than the brain.

The memorandum and the discussions that it raised delayed, but did not prevent, Ernst Bergmann's resignation from his posts in the network and from his work with the Government. He returned to the Hebrew University of Jerusalem, and there too he established a broad network of international links, far-reaching plans, new projects, and laboratories of his own. In everything he worked to the absolute limit of his extraordinary energy.

When we went to the polls in 1965, we sat down with Professor Bergmann to discuss his plans. We adopted the slogan "The scientification of Israel" and incorporated many of his ideas in our manifesto. To a considerable degree his overall scheme still guides us today in our planning for the future.

Although both demanding and imaginative in the scientific world, at home Professor Bergmann was relaxed, affable and a man of broad interests. His home—jointly created with his wife, Hani Bergmann—was a remarkable combination of her artistic tastes and his intellectual tastes. His home moved, according to the requirements of his work, from Jerusalem to Tel Aviv and back to Jerusalem. It was decorated with the finest Israeli art. With almost every visit to his home, his guests discovered a new drawing or a new picture—the Bergmanns worked very hard at encouraging artists both young and old—and beside the piano stood a collection of records of classical and modern music.

Ernst Bergmann also had a quite unique collection of books (in addition to an extensive scientific library). With books, as with people, he was adept at drawing out the remarkable and the fundamental. And his world of books only emphasized the breadth of his intellect: a combination of wisdom and faith.

From time to time he would lend me books that were not available in the usual catalogues, and that it was a rare experience to read.

One day he lent me an anthology of writings of Jewish women throughout the ages. In this book there were quotations from Hagar, Deborah and Jael, but there were also letters written by unfortunate Jewesses seized by the Sultan's eunuchs and imprisoned in his harem, pathetic appeals for help. And naturally—there were heart-rending letters from the Warsaw ghetto and the extermination camps.

On another occasion he lent me two volumes of letters exchanged between Harold Laski, the young Socialist, and Holmes, the aristocratic and conservative high court judge. These letters had been written over a period of sixteen years (between 1916 and 1932). When they began their correspondence Laski was twenty-three and Holmes seventy-five. They wrote to each other almost every day, and the main subject of their letters was the books that they had read (Laski used to read a book a day, Holmes two or three a week). These volumes are not only an anthology of philosophical books, they are an encyclopedia of wisdom, mature on one side, enthusiastic on the other—quite incomparable.

In his library there was also a wide collection of the finest artistic and literary publications, in French, English, German, and of course Hebrew. In his home there was a unique atmosphere of generous hospitality and of individualistic views on almost every subject.

Professor Bergmann did not need matches, he was a chain smoker, lighting every cigarette from the previous cigarette. He was totally indifferent to his health. When warned of the dangers of smoking, he would reply that this was "a statistical illusion" —that if, for example, a survey was to be conducted into how many chewing-gum eaters die of cancer, the conclusion would be that chewing gum also causes cancer. Anyway, he always carried boxes of matches in his pockets, and he was always quick to light other people's cigarettes. He hardly ever touched liquor—his staple drink was coffee—but here too he had unusual views of his own. "People aren't intoxicated by the drink," he claimed, "but by the smell. When a man has a cold, for example, he hardly ever gets drunk no matter how much he drinks."

His home attracted many visitors, the cream of Jerusalem's intellectual society, scientists from all over Israel and many assorted visitors from overseas. The Bergmanns had wide-ranging links with people all over the world. These links made a valuable contribution both to Israeli prestige and to Israeli science. "Thought," Professor Bergmann once said to me, "is not subject to tax, and international contacts require no visas."

Among the many wreaths laid at his graveside, one of the largest and most beautiful came from Taiwan. Professor Bergmann had especially close links with people in Nationalist China—ranging from Chiang Kai-Shek to university staff. He had similar links with scientific circles in France, Britain, Norway, Denmark and the United States. He was adept at representing the interests and problems of Israel, sometimes with brilliant clarity, and he could conduct such conversations calmly and smoothly, with unusual personal charm.

Toward the end of his life he suffered from a malignant disease. He bore it in stoical fashion and refused to submit to it, just as he had always refused to submit to any compulsion: pressures of time, sickness or distress. He thought and worked and enthused and encouraged, in his last days just as he had in his prime, with a cavalier disregard for the laws of nature until those laws finally triumphed.

With his death we lost a great creator—a creator such as only the real suffering of a people and the noble forces latent in their historical spirit can bring out into the light of day, into a world which he strove to change, to enrich, a world which he challenged in his own quiet way. The echo of this challenge is still clearly to be heard, in our generation and perhaps in future generations too. The scion of an eminent rabbinical family became a teacher to a generation of scientists.

MOSHE HAVIV
Advocate for All Men, Scourge of All Injustice

As by name—"Haviv" *—so by nature;
whoever was privileged to know him
closely will confirm that this was his chosen path.*

A FRIEND

I FIRST BECAME CLOSELY ACQUAINTED with Moshe
Haviv at the time of the formation of Rafi. We held
a meeting attended by some thirty or forty colleagues at Ben-Gurion's house in Keren Kayemet
Boulevard, and our hearts were torn. To leave the
party of which we had been members for so many
years; to leave it on account of the "Lavon Affair"

---

* "Haviv"—kind, gentle, affectionate and friendly.

—an issue on which we were far from being unanimous; to part company with colleagues and close friends who had decided not to join us; to take the field with such an impromptu force, without organization, without resources, without prior reconnaissance, to go to war against the establishment and demand its reform—it all seemed too hasty, too rash, a gesture of protest with no prospect of success.

Ben-Gurion stood firm, his mood tense and belligerent. He called me to one side and said: "If Moshe [Dayan] and you, or either of you, come with me—I shall go." Moshe was undecided, and I had serious doubts although I knew for a fact that I would never desert Ben-Gurion.

The atmosphere in Ben-Gurion's house was extremely militant. Uncertainty sounded like treachery, diffidence was interpreted as regret. Nobody smiled in that house that evening, everyone was keyed up to the limit. I myself was in a state of great confusion. Suddenly Ben-Gurion took over the chairmanship of the meeting from me and began to announce the decisions of the committee. I was offended and annoyed. I looked around me, searching for a foothold, some fixed point to which I could cling to avoid being dragged down into what seemed to me like utter madness. And then my eyes met those of Mosh Haviv. I could see that he understood my discomfort. He came to me and said softly: "If you go . . . we go."

Ben-Gurion's proclamation was unequivocal: we should establish a new independent party to compete in the sixth Knesset elections, in November 1965.

The next day Ben-Gurion returned to Sdeh Boker. Yosef Almogi was ill. Moshe Dayan was absent. How were we to start a revolt? How were we to start a movement for reform?

A friend put at our disposal two or three rooms in a building in the center of the city, but the rooms were unfurnished and empty—as were our pockets. Gradually things began to arrive: one lady brought two stools from her house, another provided curtains; somebody brought a Chagall print—two green doves on a light blue background; a husband and wife, both lawyers, offered their services as drivers —they had a car!

At about midday "Mosh" appeared. And immediately the atmosphere changed from one extreme to the other. "There's nothing to worry about," he said. "Let's go and sort out the branches." We asked him which "branches" he meant—we did not have a single one! "Ah, is that so? Well then, let's go and set them up."

The few of us who were present smiled doubtfully. Everything seemed so bizarre, so unreal. I thought to myself how appropriate it was that a strange situation should draw strange people together. Mosh too was a man who defied definition. He was neither Ashkenazi nor Sephardi, he was of Turkish origin. He was neither "egghead" nor "pragmatist," he was a lawyer by profession. He was neither optimist nor pessimist, he was, quite simply, lively and intelligent. He was so different from the rest of us—in his dress, his car, his way of speaking. And yet he seemed to us so close, so straightforward, a real member of the family.

Even before we knew what kind of a man he was, we revealed to him our most intimate secrets. His resourcefulness was intoxicating in its effects— when he advised, all complications melted into nothing; when he preached, all sobriety was swept away. People were devoted to him even before they knew him personally, they sought his friendship without knowing why he inspired such unlimited trust.

In the early days of the formation of Rafi, I was afraid that in him we might have acquired a charismatic "fellow-traveler," a man of great charm but essentially only an amateur who had decided to spend his spare time in the company of a loosely-knit group of radical agitators. It was not long before Mosh was the brightest hope of the new movement.

He did not push himself into any post, any committee. In fact he avoided all appointments and institutions. For him, any official designation was like a cage in which he was careful not to be trapped, even if the bars were made of silver. And yet, even without a title he was a central figure, an institution in his own right.

As I observed his actions I came to understand that changes begin to come about the moment that new and original people set their shoulders to the task. Every change starts with its protagonists—

with their power to mobilize resources that convention and officialdom are incapable of discovering and setting in motion.

It turned out that Mosh could do anything: a book needed publishing—he was the publisher; there was a lawsuit to be contested—he was the advocate; funds had to be raised—he organized it; colleagues became estranged—he conciliated them; branches needed opening—he founded them; a speech had to be made—Mosh dazzled his audience; somebody needed a heart-to-heart talk—Mosh could spare the time.

And moreover it became clear that Mosh was asking for nothing in return, he needed nothing: he had a senior rank in the army, he had an income, he had a car, he had an office, he was educated. In addition, he had friends, influence, a gift for words, time to spare, an equable temperament and a warm and comfortable house. Most important of all, he had a deep and sincere motivation in all his actions.

Mosh fell on the last day of the Six Day War, in the Golan Heights, when a shell struck his half-track. After his death his many friends came together to share their memories of him. And we all concluded that behind his flamboyant and charming exterior lay a firm and resolute personality, a devotion to the cause and above all else a love of humanity.

A friend asked him to draw up a contract for the purchase of a house, and Mosh discovered that his friend had miscalculated and was several thousand pounds short; he drew up the contract and without saying a word he wrote him a check for the amount required. The man had not asked for it, and Mosh was not rich. A friend found himself with nowhere to sleep; Mosh offered him his bed. A friend was discharged from the army with no job to go to; Mosh offered him a share in his business. A friend had problems in his private life; Mosh came to his aid immediately. His door was always open to those in need. He studied law so that he could be an advocate for all men. He did not speak loftily about "humanity" as something distant and abstract; he was concerned with people whom he knew, whom he saw, who needed understanding or assistance.

Mosh was born in Istanbul, and when he was about four years old his parents decided to emigrate to Palestine. After spending a year on the island of Rhodes they settled in Jerusalem in 1935. He began his education at the Convent School of St. Joseph, and went on from there to the Alliance School.

While a pupil at the High School he joined the Gadna (a paramilitary youth movement), and in the twelfth grade he organized a students' "revolt": he set up a private "broadcasting station" in his home and called upon his young friends to demand early enlistment in the Haganah. The revolt was a success and the matriculation examinations were brought forward for the whole class.

In 1948 Mosh joined the Palmach and went with a scout group to settle on a kibbutz. From there he went on a platoon-commanders' course in Kibbutz Dalia. With the outbreak of the War of Independence, on his own initiative he went down to the Negev with a number of friends and joined the Seventh Brigade of the Palmach. As a company commander Mosh was involved in the attacks on Iraq el Manshie, Sueidan and Huleikat. Later, leading a contingent of recent immigrants, he took part in the conquest of Beersheba and the opening of the road to S'dom.

After "Operation Horev," in which he also participated, he was sent to an officers' school near Netanya. At the age of twenty he was a captain, and at twenty-one he was the youngest major in the IDF. In 1952 he was appointed commander of the Gadna in the Jerusalem area, a post giving ample scope to his organizational skills and good temper. He organized a number of different activities, ranging from a hike to Jerusalem in which about a thousand people took part, to projects aimed at helping urban youth and young delinquents.

While still in uniform he enrolled at the Hebrew University of Jerusalem, studied law and qualified as a lawyer. Having completed his studies he went on a paratroopers' course and earned his "wings."

For a short time he directed Beit Zvi * in Ramat Gan, before joining a legal firm in Tel Aviv. At the beginning of the sixties he was appointed legal adviser to Mapai, an appointment which terminated when he joined the group, led by Ben-Gurion, which set out to campaign for justice in political life.

He had a passion for justice. All his life was

---

* A theater school.

spent in one great lawsuit. He took up arms against the negative side of our lives, against injustice, idleness and corruption.

Once on a trip to Masada, a few tough youngsters split away from the main party on account of the heat and the thirst and went off by themselves in search of rest and refreshment. Mosh and Gulliver —himself one of our country's finest sons—set out in pursuit, caught the young men and thrashed them soundly. On another occasion, when a camp commander deprived the men on a training course of the leave that was due to them, Mosh organized a revolt.

When men of the Palmach were critical of Ben-Gurion's decision to disband the Palmach command, Mosh suggested that a public trial be held and he volunteered to represent Ben-Gurion—the only man in the camp prepared to do so. Some years later he really did represent him, and his colleagues, in a different episode.

He loved freedom. He was not attracted to profit. Restrictions were anathema to him and institutions depressed him. Conventional obligations inspired his imagination—to find a way out of them. It was as if every morning he wanted to be born anew, to meet a friend, to tour the country, to drive fast, to fulfill a duty, to repair a wrong, and to be himself—charming, sincere and a help to others, following his inclinations freely, guiding by instinct his dazzling intellect. No menu, no bill, no binding obligation, no contrived conception of duty, a personality with wings and a love of flying, loving to help others to be as free as himself.

Always free, but never unreliable. He was the first to respond to every appeal, explicit or implicit. He was the first to volunteer for any service. And just as there was no idea above his understanding, there was no task beneath his dignity.

When we decided to form an independent list, in the latter half of 1965, we called ourselves Rafi—Reshimat Poaley Yisrael (Israeli Workers' List). Officially we had not yet split from Mapai, which is why we made the distinction between a list and a party, considering that "list" has a certain ad hoc flavor to it, it suggests protest but it is still an option, whereas "party" implies a final decision; we considered that the difference between the two was like the difference between separation and divorce. And then the party decided to bring us before a party tribunal. Picked out as defendants were David Ben-Gurion, Yizhar Smilansky, Amos Dagani, Gideon Ben-Yisrael, Hannah Lamdan, Yosef Almogi, David Lipschitz and myself.

At first the party had difficulty appointing judges. Who would countenance the prospect of sitting in judgment on David Ben-Gurion? It was only after a great deal of effort that a panel of judges was appointed, and they were: the lawyer David Harman; Zvi Rechter, from Solel Boneh; Yehiel Duvdevani, from Mekorot; Michael Assaf from Davar; and Meir Ben-Meir, from the Beersheba branch. Counsel for the prosecution were two eminent veteran party members: Yaakov Shimshon Shapiro, later to become Minister of Justice, and Nahum Shadmi, a veteran of the Haganah and head of the party's research department.

Our group, the defendants, looked around for advocates—men without fear, who would be prepared to give up their time for no financial reward. The two who agreed were Micha Caspi, a distinguished and eminent lawyer, who took on the task of defending Ben-Gurion, and naturally enough, Mosh, who was to represent the whole group.

Mosh called me and said: "We must coordinate our tactics with the 'Old Man.' " I felt uncomfortable. Firstly, "coordinating" anything with Ben-Gurion seemed to me an impossible dream; this great and impetuous man, with his lust for battle and his conviction that he was in the right—how could anything be coordinated with him? Secondly, the word "tactics" seemed to me out of place; Ben-Gurion, although he had once studied law himself, certainly did not see the impending suit as a question of "tactics." But the very idea of introducing Mosh to Ben-Gurion and having them work together appealed to me very strongly. I was sure that the two men would find a great deal in common.

Once again the whole group met in Ben-Gurion's house, on the open balcony, under the dubious eye of Paula. Ben-Gurion was in a relaxed mood. "What's it all about?" he asked. I said: "Mosh, say your piece."

Mosh spoke, roughly as follows: "Look, Ben-

Gurion, in a few days' time the lawsuit against you and against us will begin. We must decide on the line that we shall take."

Ben-Gurion stopped him there: "What do you suggest?"

"That instead of defending ourselves we attack the party. I suggest that there should be no technical argument over our right to split from the party; we should turn the courtroom into a public stage, from which we can make known to the public our objections to what is going on in the party, to the misuse of power, to deceit, to the miscarriages of justice in the Lavon case."

Ben-Gurion looked with great curiosity at the young man—Mosh looked younger than he really was—with the sparkling eyes and the clear and bold tongue. "What is your name?" he asked. Before Mosh could answer, somebody shouted: "Mosh Haviv."

"Mosh? What kind of a name is that, Mosh? They should have called you Moshe." Mosh smiled broadly and replied: "Ben-Gurion, you will soon see the difference between Moshe and Mosh."

Du Sublime au ridicule il n'ay a qu'un pas: the French proverb is an apt description of the lawsuit that was brought against us. A group of men who owed their careers to Ben-Gurion's help and patronage had decided to expel from their ranks the founder of the party, its guide, its formal and spiritual leader.

Hardly a single one of his veteran comrades

stood by Ben-Gurion. His support came from younger men, at the outset of their careers, men motivated by enthusiasm for change and personal loyalty to Ben-Gurion.

The case was heard in Mapai headquarters, in Hayarkon Street, Tel Aviv. Not long ago this had been our own headquarters, now it had become the dock in a trial whose result was a foregone conclusion. In front of the building we were greeted by a crowd of our supporters carrying placards which read "The Trial of Socrates."

We took our places behind the specially erected partition, Micha Caspi and Mosh at our head. Micha had equipped himself with a mass of material regarding the constitution and the rules of the party, and he was determined not to give way on a single legal point. Mosh watched with eagle eye every move on the part of the prosecution. When he felt that Yaakov Shimshon Shapiro was being unduly provocative, he instructed us to keep cool and not to react to such challenges. Indeed, when Shapiro called Ben-Gurion a coward and there was uproar in the courtroom, Ben-Gurion replied with the request that he be treated like anyone else and added nothing further.

Mosh's other piece of advice was also followed: the defendant's box became the plaintiff's stand. Ben-Gurion's testimony was full of sharp-edged remarks, many of them with a prophetic ring:

> If the Party leadership succeeds in expelling me from the Party, it will make no

difference to me, I have never regarded the framework of the Party as something sacred in its own right; a party is only as good as the values that it stands for, that it puts into practice. . . . Even if they expel me from the Party, to my last breath I shall never abandon the fight for the values, moral, pioneering and political, to which I have dedicated my life, and if the Party framework is damaged beyond hope of repair, then I shall choose the values rather than the Party. . . . A majority at the Conference and in the Mapai central leadership, which a few months ago fell under the control of a regime of fear and deceit, is not the whole of the people, nor is it the whole of the working class.

And we, the rest of the defendants, were no less outspoken. When I showed Mosh the draft of my statement he advised me: "When you sharpen your sword blunt your oratory." I followed his advice, and among other things, I said:

And so, to my sorrow I am obliged to call into question the very authority of this court to judge the case under discussion, since there is no body of law, no objective judiciary, on the basis of which a judgment may be reached; the process that has preceded the hearing itself has been tainted with errors of both omission and commission, it has run counter to the entire constitution of the Party. The institutions that

have prepared this action are institutions
that should themselves be brought before a
Party tribunal, on account of their inconsis-
tent behavior and their corruption of the
rationale of the movement into ephemeral
and antimovement interests. Allow me to
explain more fully.

The situation that has been created in
Mapai in 1965 has no precedent in reality
and no basis in Party rules. In fact, Mapai is
not going to the polls at all; a section of the
members of Mapai is standing under the
title "United Israeli Workers' List" together
with another section which calls itself "Israeli Workers' List." And it is hard to decide
which "list" is more faithful to the path of
Mapai, the plaintiff or the defendant. . . .

The stand that we took forced the prosecution
to sharpen its tone. Even Nahum Shadmi, that most
moderate of men, could not restrain himself from
saying: "It is a disaster for both Party and people,
when we see signs of dictatorial tendencies in one of
its greatest sons." Yaakov Shimshon Shapiro went
even further, calling Gideon Ben-Yisrael a neo-fas-
cist; this outburst was to haunt him throughout his
many years in public life.

There were no surprises in the performance of
Micha Caspi—he was an eminent legal expert of
long standing. But Mosh, the effervescent and
barely-known individualist, made his reputation in
this case, not only as a skilled and experienced law-

yer, but also as a man of true legal temperament, keeping calm and not flying off at a tangent, using only prearranged arguments whose effectiveness was assured.

It seems that in his heart Mosh preferred trial drama to the conventions imposed by the party framework. He was afraid that with the passage of time this framework would turn into an oligarchy, a small ruling clique growing ever more exclusive and tenacious; the great ideals that had created it would gradually become a necessary convention and would ultimately lead to bad practices, habits hard to break. Individual freedom was becoming an endless series of obligations, from which it followed that a man going out to search for new freedom would only succeed in creating a new captivity for himself. The young men, who in the meantime were growing older, were taking all the key positions, and there was no longer any opportunity for the really young men who would follow them.

Law is not like that. Before the law all men are equal. Both the lonely man and the simple man can find an advocate. A man who hates falsehood can set himself up as a prosecutor and make a positive contribution to its correction. He is not committed to a foreordained social convention; his only duty is to put his case courageously, to examine both sides of the coin, dismissing one and insisting on the other. Moreover, a man can lay accusations against his colleague without being or becoming his enemy, the result that logically could be expected; conversely a man can defend his colleague without identifying totally with his client's point of view, and without being dazzled by the weight of arguments that he has amassed in his professional capacity.

Mosh preferred the lawyer's stand to the chair of authority. In the lawsuit involving Ben-Gurion and his colleagues, he was fortunate in that on this occasion he was able to pronounce and express his political opinions within the context of the legal arena; he was in a position to defend a man whom he admired in a setting where the rules of defense counted for more than the degree of admiration.

On his advice, we asked permission to call as witnesses the leaders of Mapai, including Eshkol and Golda. The court refused our request. Then we decided to have nothing more to do with the proceedings, "since we have been prevented from calling witnesses whose testimony, in describing the background to the course of events that led finally to the split in Mapai, is vital to the defense."

The verdict, delivered on September 2, 1965, surprised nobody. It stated that it was the defendants who had split from Mapai, and therefore they were no longer to be considered members of that party; the court also dissociated itself from the recriminations voiced during the trial—expressions such as "cowardice," "deceit" and "neo-fascists."

Whenever we were in difficulty, we turned to Mosh.

One day we received an invitation from Rivka

Guber, a wonderful woman who had lost both her sons but refused to bow to her bitter fate. She had gone to live near Lachish where she participated in creating a new settlement and helped educate young people of the area. Rivka was a close friend of Ben-Gurion and she had been one of the founder members of Rafi; her husband, Mordecai, had decided to stay in Mapai since, although his views were close to those of Rivka, he disapproved of the split. Rivka invited us to a meeting in Nehora where a vigorous debate was expected, not only between friends but between members of the same family.

I respected the Guber family, and I felt uneasy about becoming involved in such a controversial issue at a meeting attended by both Mordecai and Rivka. At the last moment I had an inspiration: I would invite Mosh! With him it would be impossible to go wrong. He would find the right tone, the most convincing argument, without leaving behind the slightest trace of bad taste.

When I spoke to Mosh on the telephone and explained what it was all about, he replied, in characteristic vein: "It's a pity you're not inviting me just four or five hours in advance. Surely you could have asked me at the last moment. Of course I'll come with you."

We arrived in Nehora on a cold winter night, wrapped up in sweaters and overcoats and secretly hoping that the weather would keep the audience away. But we were mistaken. The community center was packed. Rivka, who was to chair the proceedings, greeted us with a bouquet of roses, still dripping with rainwater.

I looked at the audience, then I looked at Mosh and asked him to begin. A murmur of surprise passed through the hall—who was this man? But within the space of a few minutes it was clear that all those present had fallen under the spell of his passionate eloquence, his flawless logic, the delicate touches of humor that held his arguments together.

This was one of the most remarkable speeches that I ever heard. Mosh knew that most of the audience, like Mordecai, sympathized with the radical principles of Rafi, but either had doubts on the issue of the separate list or were totally opposed to it. He decided to resolve this doubt with a simile of his own: "It does not matter what it is that brings a child into the world—it may be marriage, it may be love, it may be chance, it may even be a mistake. But once the child is born it makes no difference how he first saw the light of day. He lives and exists, he breathes and grows. The reason for his birth is immaterial compared with the fact of his existence. It may be that some of you think that the formation of Rafi was the product of chance, or even a mistake, but such considerations have no further relevance. It is a living, existing, fighting body. . . ."

Mosh continued: "Moreover, the creation of Rafi provides an answer to the question which is troubling many people: what is the best method of fighting the corruption which has become endemic in our movement on account of the consolidation of power in the hands of the ruling clique and the perversion of electoral procedures. A weapon for the fight has been created. And it has been created because the lines have been drawn and a battle is inevitable. . . ." Mosh went on to explain that young people would be betraying their generation if they chose the way of compromise and not the way of change, "Walking in the furrow, instead of clearing a new field." When he finished his speech there was a storm of applause. A man sitting next to me turned to me and asked: "Where have you been hiding him all this time?"

Rafi had men of ideas, but very few men of means; and without means it is impossible to build up a movement and impossible to fight an election campaign. Mosh willingly took upon himself the difficult task of acquiring funds. After some time he came up with an idea: we would set up our own publishing company! I had no idea what the business involved and how we would benefit from it, but if Mosh suggested it—it was worth trying.

We decided to publish, as our first venture, a commemorative album in honor of Ben-Gurion's eightieth birthday, in Hebrew and English. An English version was clearly impossible without the cooperation of an American publisher. Somebody would have to go to the United States.

Mosh set out on his mission knowing nothing at all about the American publishing business, without contacts or letters of introduction. He had just one week at his disposal. After one week exactly he arrived back in Israel, accompanied by an American publisher.

The latter proved to be a most interesting person, an experienced publisher and a man of refined taste. He was fascinated by the project and agreed to publish our album, on condition that it was ready *within six weeks*. Mosh said to me: "Agree to it, Shimon, we can do it."

That evening we held a meeting in my house. Four of our colleagues, men with experience of the publishing trade, expressed a unanimous decision: six weeks—impossible! But Mosh was not the kind to accept the conventional as inevitable. He set out to convince us that it was indeed possible, and whenever anyone showed signs of losing patience, Mosh glanced at him as if to say: "Leave it to me, I'll sort it out."

The next morning we all set to work feverishly, while Mosh stood behind us brandishing the whip of his charm. Within six weeks the album was ready to go to press. The printed edition was a work of the highest taste, although the revenue from it barely covered the cost of production.

More than once I have asked myself the question: how often in life do you meet a man like Mosh? A soldier and an officer, a colleague and a leader, a man who gave freely to society, a stunning orator, a resourceful man for whom no task is too difficult, and in addition to all this—a man liked by all those who come into contact with him. I have heard criticism of him, but never have I encountered hostility toward him.

He never benefited from nepotism or preferential treatment. Nothing came to him by chance, nothing was ever handed to him on a plate. He was a self-made man, personally responsible for his education, his character, the tasks entrusted to him. He never stood to the side. However difficult the mission he knew how to choose the right time to approach it and he played a truly vital role in grappling with it.

On the eve of the Six Day War we met—Gad Yaakobi, Mosh and I. Mosh said: "Look, we went to war in 1947–48, and again in 1956; now once more we are going out for a meeting with fate. Don't you think that it's a bit too much?"

When I heard a rumor that Mosh had fallen, I checked all the relevant data—the place, the vehicle, the number, and I knew that Mosh was indeed no more. I was overcome by a sense of loneliness such as I had not known for many years.

YONATAN NETANYAHU
First in Line and First to Fall

By "the past" I mean not only my personal past but the pattern of which I see myself as an inseparable part, as a link in the chain of our existence and the independence of Israel.

YONI

THE SABBATH OF JULY 3, 1976 was fraught with tension; only a few hours earlier, as Minister of Defense, I had driven with the Chief of Staff and senior officers to a secluded airstrip where a chosen unit, composed of volunteers, was preparing to leave. The young men, armed to the teeth, began climbing the gangways of the giant Hercules transports, engines already running, bound for a faraway destination, four thousand kilometers from home, there to tackle the unknown.

The officers and men were in high spirits, although it was clear that they were aware of the importance of the mission and the difficulty of the test that awaited them. We shook hands with the officers. They told us not to worry and strode confidently toward the aircraft. At the steps they turned back, waved their hands and disappeared into the belly of the gigantic bird.

In the morning a Government sitting had been called. The decision which was taken was in clear opposition to what had recently been the prevailing mood within the Government. For a week it had sat and debated the question of what should be done to free the passengers kidnapped in the Air France plane and flown to Entebbe in Uganda. The balance of opinion seemed to be in favor of exchanging the hostages for Fatah terrorists. As Minister of Defense I had worked with my colleagues throughout that week to find another solution—a means of freeing the kidnap victims by an armed intervention of our own.

The right decisions were needed. Even more important, the right men were needed. The success of the operation depended on the men. All that day there was radio silence. We agreed that only in the event of a hitch, or, God forbid, a catastrophe, would this silence be broken and a radio report be made.

Every moment of silence was a relief to us. The time passed slowly. At seven P.M., two minutes after the anticipated time, the radio receivers opened up and we heard the familiar and matter-of-fact voice of General Dan Shomron, the commander of the operation. He informed us laconically: "We've landed. Don't worry. If anything goes wrong—I'll let you know."

When the mission had been completed—one of the most daring operations in military history—we received a further report: "We have a casualty."

There was silence in the room. Nobody dared to ask the identity of the casualty, or what his condition was. Security considerations and premonition combined to prevent the asking of this question. There were a number of generals in the room. Two of them had sons taking part in this perilous mission. The expression on their faces did not change —at such times all men are fathers to all sons.

At three o'clock in the morning Motta Gur, the Chief of Staff, came into my room and said: "It's Yoni!" We had not speculated on the identity of the casualty when we heard the news over the airwaves, but even then we knew in our hearts that the slight tremor in the voice reporting "We have a casualty" concealed some particularly precious name. Both Motta and I felt lumps in our throats. There was nothing to add. The name Yoni said it all, it said what one of his friends, Elisha Brameir, wrote of him: "Yoni is a perpetual fight against sleep, fatigue, idleness, forgetfulness, inefficiency, helplessness, deceit. Yoni is the turning of the impossible into the possible."

Yoni was in command of the assault force at Entebbe Airport and while leading his men in the attack, he was killed by a bullet through the heart.

A week earlier I had seen him at dead of night, at a military briefing near Lod Airport. This was immediately after we heard the first reports of the hijacking of the French plane. A special unit under Yoni's command had been assembled there, so that if the need arose—that is, if the plane landed at Lod —they would be able to storm it immediately, take control of it and free the hostages.

There was a unique atmosphere at this *ad hoc* briefing. The officers gave out their instructions, and every word seemed to weigh a ton. On the walls hung diagrams of different planes, since we did not yet know what type of aircraft had been hijacked. And to the side stood models of various kinds of ladder; everything seemed precise, organized and disciplined, so military—apart, perhaps, from the young men themselves. They were bareheaded, with tousled curls. They looked so young, so serious, men who knew what lay ahead of them and were prepared to meet whatever came, with confidence, daring and expertise.

In the darkness badges of rank were invisible, but there was no need for them; you could tell who the natural leaders were, each man in his place, each man with his degree of responsibility.

Yoni was the center of the group. They turned

to him with questions and remarks, messengers came to him with reports, suggestions, new maps, psychological assessments of the likely behavior of the terrorists. I asked Yoni which he regarded as preferable: to storm the plane as soon as it touched down, or to allow it to land, enter negotiation with the terrorists, and only then decide on a course of action.

Yoni thought for a moment and gave a characteristic answer: he preferred immediate assault. He considered that both options, immediate assault and delayed assault, were equally dangerous. But if the operation were to be carried out instantly there would be the element of surprise and a greater chance of saving life.

As we were still debating this point a further report was received: the plane had diverted from its eastward course and turned south, toward Africa. The tension relaxed slightly. I could not resist asking Yoni if he knew the poetry of Alterman. He replied that his favorite book was *City of the Dove* and that Alterman was one of his two favorite poets —the other being Edgar Allan Poe.

Yoni had only a year previously been appointed commander of this unit. The appointment, considered an event of crucial importance, required meticulous consideration both at the highest level of the General Staff, and at the level of the officers and soldiers themselves. After all, it is the commander appointed to the task who is entrusted with the success of military operations sometimes involving delicate and complex political issues. It is on the commander, and his men, that the outcome of such operations depends. Furthermore, a commander lives in close proximity with his men, and his personality and resolve, his wisdom and powers of leadership, are constantly under test, hour by hour. The morale of the unit, as well as its efficiency, depends very much on the commander. Before such an appointment, the General Staff took into account not only the opinions of the candidate's superior officers, but also those of his future subordinates.

Yoni was the natural choice—an appointment welcomed both from "above" and "below." He had already proved himself in real combat, as a man of rare courage, perception and unusual intelligence.

In our army there are two kinds of report: official information, which percolates through the military hierarchy, and unofficial information, which spreads through the ranks. The first determines a man's rank, the second, his status.

Through unofficial channels such as these, the Netanyahu family had already gained an almost legendary status. Three brothers, all of them volunteers and courageous fighters, who with their valor and leadership had scored some remarkable achievements. Their reputation had preceded the official reports on them. And Yoni, the eldest among them, a fearless officer who seemed destined for promotion to the highest ranks of the IDF. And his personality was augmented not only by the charm of the hero, but also by the charms of poetry and philosophy. His appearance fitted his image: a statuesque young man, reticent of speech, with a tousled head and fine features—a personality inspiring trust and radiating good will.

A squad consists of men and minds. Such a squad cannot rely solely on the weapons and the equipment at its disposal, or on the training that it has undergone. The true basis of the unit is the man, every single man. And all together. The first, sometimes the decisive duty of the commander, is to choose his man. An officer may be judged by the quality of his choice. When a unit has a reputation, the best young men are drawn toward it. The commander must pick one from among ten or twenty volunteers, all of whom are of excellent quality. Its essential principles are reticence, which suits the nature of its operations, and modesty, which is reflected in the style of the men. The slightest boast would mean immediate expulsion from the unit. Yoni himself maintained this rule, saying to the men under his command: "I believe that the danger facing a unit is that of falling into personal complacency. I would like the men of this unit always to feel a slight sense of concern, wondering if there is something more that we can achieve, or improve."

The volunteers naturally undergo physical and psychological tests, but they must also show special qualities that are not recorded in the manual and that cannot be measured. It is these special qualities which turn a good soldier into an exceptional one. The commander must, therefore, be sharp-eyed and

capable of judging people, an expert in the discovery
of high ability and top potential. There is nothing
tangible about this, but the men themselves know if
their commander "has got eyes in his head" and has
the kind of intuition that enables him to make the
right judgments.

Deep knowledge and understanding of the
human mind are things which a commander must
show not only in regard to his own men. He must
apply the same human understanding to men whom
he does not know personally: the enemy. At the
crucial moment it is not only a question of who will
draw his weapon and fire first, but of who will cor-
rectly anticipate the behavior of his own men and
his opponents.

"Over a period of more than a year," Yoni told
his men, "during which I have commanded this brigade, I have watched you growing and growing up, I
have seen with pleasure the formation of a healthy
backbone of regular soldiers—NCOs and officers—
within the brigade. I have watched the brigade pro-
gressing from week to week and not resting on its
laurels, I have seen you, men and officers, achieving
good results and always forging ahead. . . ." This is
how he saw his men while his men were in a position to judge him when there was an enemy to con-
tend with. They saw him in action, rallying his
troops and leading them into the attack, making the
right decisions and getting the better of forces nu-
merically superior to his own. The conflict between
David and Goliath also had a spiritual dimension,

and it may be that through this dimension the outcome of the struggle was determined from the start.

But an understanding of people is not enough. The operations in which his unit took part demanded a broad fundamental knowledge, expertise of the very highest order. Yoni maintained this principle very strongly: "I believe in getting down to the most minute details. Anyone who omits to do this in the hope of saving effort will fail in his primary objective—to prepare his men for battle."

The officers of this unit studied maps as their forefathers had studied the pages of the Talmud—every contour line and every concealed gully was studied intently, for hidden creases, an unknown face, an unmarked possibility.

The light of day is for the delicate. The field of vision and action of such men as these is the night, from before moonrise till dawn. Agreeable weather is not to be relied on, the unit is capable of operating in heavy rain, in wind and in stormy seas. Vegetation can conceal the enemy. It can also provide camouflage for your own troops; it has to be studied, examined and exploited for the maximum effect.

From the starting point to the objective the map is studied endlessly, until it has been digested and its contents can be recited by heart. Slowly a tapestry of action is evolved, detailed expertise joining forces with a novelty that defies experience.

And then comes the greatest demand on the soldiers themselves: backbreaking training, water discipline and food discipline, long route marches in harsh climatic conditions, carrying heavy equipment, and every time there is a fresh attempt at attaining better results. There is a continuous and unflagging attention paid to each and every detail. "I believe," said Yoni to his men, "that there is no compromising with results. In this brigade, let us never be content with results that are not the best possible. Even the best possible can be further improved and enhanced."

And even after the soldiers have been trained up to scratch, and the plan has been worked out and all is prepared for action, it is still the job of the officers of the unit—the commander first and foremost—to convince his superiors that the plan is feasible and potentially successful.

The "top brass" are full of admiration for the unit and they have no doubt of its ability. But they feel a certain anxiety: perhaps the young men are again taking on themselves too rash an operation, for which they will have to pay too high a price, both in qualitative and quantitative terms. Their very readiness to sacrifice themselves, and their aptitude for dealing with difficult circumstances are a cause for doubt, a fear that they may be taking on more than is reasonable, more than is possible.

Yoni was an expert in these things. By nature he was a man of truth, a strict adherer to the truth. In addition to this he was a master of invention and surprises and capable of expressing himself lucidly. He was not the type to underestimate problems; he spoke with sober realism. The imagination in his approach was a product of the aptitude for interpretation which is so great a part of the reality of our lives. Yoni succeeded in earning the confidence of both his men and his superiors. The plan was approved.

It is then that the moment of greatest loneliness comes. All the preparations and the training—all these are now subjected to the moment of fearful truth, a moment in which life and death are separated by the merest hair's-breadth. Every battle is a kind of test, in which the unpredictable must be expected. The operation is performed at giddy speed, controlled by the briefest orders and sometimes by signals and gestures alone. With eyes wide open and ears receptive to the slightest sound, the commander must remain in calm control of the entire operation. Within seconds he must decide which is the strong point, which is the weak, and to whom the crucial missions should be entrusted; and all these decisions have to be taken, sometimes under heavy fire, sometimes in total silence, usually in a flood of surprises. He stands like the conductor of an orchestra, directing fire this way and that, and there is nobody who can advise him. He is the ultimate authority on the spot. If his conducting is a success, it means victory; if it fails, it is defeat. As Yoni himself said: "There is no compromising with results."

So it was with "Operation Yonatan" at Entebbe. For the few days and nights available to them, the young men trained without a break under their conductor's baton. A replica of Entebbe Airport was constructed, and every detail of the place was studied. On the map, which covered a range of four thousand kilometers, every square was examined. A study was made of weather conditions along the flight path, of the range of the radar screens and of the most economical flying altitude. Seating positions in the planes were allocated and the order of assault determined. A special medical unit was prepared, emergency landing sites decided on, and a plan devised for the extrication of the hostages. The whole operation was planned to the second, from the second of landing to the second of takeoff. The planners worked in close liaison with the Air Force personnel, whose part in the operation would be decisive from the moment of takeoff onward and much was dependent on the pilots, on their courage and expertise.

On the eve of the operation we received information that Idi Amin had gone abroad, and that he was due to return to Uganda on the Saturday evening, at the exact time that the operation would probably be starting in earnest. With this in mind the soldiers decided to make an Idi Amin of their own. . . .

Idi Amin would be driven in a Mercedes, a Mercedes identical to his real one. The particulars of all the Mercedes cars in Israel were fed into a computer—Idi Amin only drives in the most expensive of them. And when a car similar to his was identified, it was found that it was light in color, whereas Idi's was black. Yoni and his men set to work on the car; the day before the Operation they managed to paint it black and the Mercedes came off the plane at Entebbe with one of the soldiers playing the role of Idi Amin at the wheel, to add to the surprise and the confusion. Indeed, this idea and its execution were typical of the unit and its commander; they could turn their hands to anything, with an initiative equal to their courage, and both these qualities—initiative and courage—had the effect of reducing their dependence on luck and chance.

The operation began two minutes late, but it was completed four minutes ahead of schedule. The passengers and crew members were rescued. The terrorists—Arab and German—were killed. Idi Amin, who had hoped to stage a grandiose theatrical performance for the benefit of world public opinion, lost this round of the game, earning only ridicule and shame.

This was in the morning of July 4. In the United States, jubilation at the victory was combined with the celebration of Independence Day. The whole world gaped in astonishment at the news of this operation, which had gone beyond the bounds of the imagination.

We drove to a military airbase in the south to welcome the soldeirs and the rescued hostages. The first to step from the plane was Yoni's deputy, who has assumed command from the moment that the leader fell. He gave a brief instruction: Yoni first, then the severely wounded paratrooper.

When asked how it happened he replied simply: "He was first in line and the first to fall."

Later Yoni's deputy described the operation in a short and moving broadcast on the IDF radio station. His report included the following extracts:

"Yoni went over the whole of the plan for the operation in detail. I have to say that throughout the preparation stage he was in a state of unusual excitement, and unlike the rest of us he was quite sure that the operation would go ahead and the plan would finally be approved.

"Yoni was very tired—in fact, all the officers and men in the squad were worn out from the exertions of the previous week. So I suggested at one point that we give ourselves a break and get some sleep. This was at about two or three A.M. on the Friday. Yoni agreed and the men dispersed, but later we discovered that he had stayed on alone in his office and continued with the final preparations. And when he presented the plan at seven in the morning, after sleeping for an hour or two at the most, I remembered the plan as we had left it before, and I discovered that Yoni had added a number of new and ingenious points. The plan that he presented that morning was perfect and complete in every detail.

"We carried on with our training and exercises, with Yoni coordinating everything personally. I should point out that it is at such times as these that the commander is subjected to his severest test. The test is especially severe when he is also under endless pressure from the General Staff to prove the validity of his plan.

"Yoni was obliged to supervise the training and ensure that everything was worked out to the last detail, and in addition to 'sell' his plan to higher authority. All these things add up to tremendous pressure. And Yoni stood up to it wonderfully. He was calm and relaxed, directing everything in an orderly fashion, and noting everything down in his clear handwriting. At one stage we advised him to leave us to carry on with the training and the exercises, and concentrate on the task of persuading his superiors. He rejected this advice and insisted on supervising the training personally.

"Before we embarked on the plane Yoni gave his final instructions. He wanted to be sure that everyone was fully briefed and knew exactly what had to be done.

"In the plane we were in excellent spirits. He laughed and joked. An hour before we were due to land he roused us and shook hands with the junior officers. . . .

"Here I should point out that Yoni was one of the most courageous men I have ever known. I have seen him in action in a great many battles, in the war and in other operations. He always stood by the principle 'The commander leads the attack.' I well remember the battle near Nafah, in the Yom Kippur War. My most vivid memory of this battle is of Yoni leading an assault with eight men against twelve Syrian commandos and killing them all. This is a scene that I shall never forget: Yoni attacking, shooting and leading his men into battle, leading them, not giving orders from behind.

"For this reason one of the officers approached him in the plane and said: 'Remember that you're in command. You mustn't be injured. Keep a safe distance and don't get too close to the assault party.' I saw Yoni smile, grip his hand and say that it would be all right. As it turned out, in this battle too Yoni was in the ideal commander's position, from which he could watch the progress of the battle and take immediate action in the event of complications (if someone is injured, for example). From the point of view of personal safety this was obviously the most dangerous position for an officer, because it was close to the action taking place. Yoni chose the position which was most dangerous, but also most influential and decisive."

In the "ideal position" the "most influential position" and the "most dangerous position," Yoni fell in the flower of his youth, and with his death the nation was made aware of a hitherto unknown figure, a man both bold and profound, one of the most eminent of his generation, and one of Israel's finest sons.

Yoni's father is an historian and a philosopher. His grandfather Vilokevsky published some important works of biblical studies. In different circumstances Yoni would certainly have followed in the footsteps of his forefathers, in the great cultural heritage of the Jewish people. But in his own way, he was filled with this cultural spirit.

To a colleague at Harvard he said: "The present crisis is military. But the future crisis will be diplomatic." This brief statement expresses Israel's situation in a nutshell.

In one of the letters he wrote with a poet's pen: "My way shall pass through fertile pastures, through pleasant gardens, among mountains and cliffs and deserts, but in all its windings it will follow that path which is both familiar and mysterious." And in another letter: "We are all searching for another place, a beautiful place, where waking up is worthwhile."

As a boy of seventeen he wrote: "I must feel that not only at the moment of my death will I be able to render an account of the time which I have lived, but that at every moment of my life I can look myself in the face and say—thus and thus have I done."

The grief which descended on the nation on the day of Yoni's funeral was no less profound than the sense of pride inspired by the operation, the operation which Yoni commanded and led, the operation which restored the belief in our own strength.

Beside his freshly dug grave, beside his mother, his father and his brothers, I took my final leave of him. And this is what I said:

"The Entebbe Raid was an operation unique in military history. It proved that Israel is capable not only of maintaining defensible frontiers, but also of taking decisive action in defense of her interests. Against a background of international terrorism of the most extreme kind, terrorism aided and abetted by the army and the President of Uganda, at a distance of more than four thousand kilometers from home, in one short hour, the stature of the Jewish people was enhanced—as was the stature of free and responsible people throughout the world.

"This operation involved the taking of a great risk—a risk that was judged preferable to the alternative, the risk of giving in to terrorists and kidnappers, of coming to terms with them.

"The hardest moment on this night of heroism came when we heard that a bullet had claimed the life of one of the finest sons of our nation, one of the most valiant Israeli warriors, one of our army's most promising commanders—the heroic Yonatan Netanyahu.

"I saw him just a few nights beforehand, at a field headquarters, preparing the men under his command for an action of a quite different kind, which then seemed a possibility. He was as calm and relaxed as usual, a natural field commander. When this handsome fellow assumed command of his squad, we recognized in him an officer of the highest quality. He was more than equal to the heavy responsibilities laid upon him, and his men turned night into day in their efforts to bring deliverance to our nation.

"What did we not lay on the shoulders of Yonatan and his comrades? The hardest assignment ever entrusted to the IDF; the most daring of its missions; the actions furthest from home and nearest to the enemy; the darkness of the night and the loneliness of the soldier; the encounter with the unknown, and the danger which is as real in peacetime as in war.

"It happens sometimes that the fate of the people is entrusted to a handful of soldiers and volunteers. For one brief hour they hold the keys to our survival. There is nobody else to consult, nowhere else to turn—the commanders on the spot determine the outcome of the battle.

"The basic logic of the Entebbe Raid was the rescue, by force of Israeli arms, of passengers whom Arabs and Germans had marked down as hostages for the sole reason that they were Israeli Jews.

"Yoni was the commander of the force entrusted with the rescue mission, and it was no accident that he was chosen for the task. He was already known for his courage and determination in rescue operations. In the citation for the medal that was awarded to him it was said: 'When a senior officer was wounded at Tel-Shams, Major Yonatan Netanyahu volunteered to lead the rescue party—after a previous attempt had failed—and succeeded in this mission; with his courage, speed of action and devotion of duty he set an example to his men.'

"Yonatan was indeed an exemplary officer. With his daring he was more than a match for his enemies. With his charm he won the hearts of his comrades. He was steadfast in peril and modest in victory. He demanded much from himself, and to the army he gave the sharpness of his mind, his operational skill, his energy in combat.

"At university he studied philosophy. In the army he was a volunteer and taught others to volunteer. To his subordinates he gave the warmth of his personality, and on the battlefield he inspired confidence.

"This young man was among the commanders of an operation quite without flaw, and yet his was a sacrifice of unprecedented pain—the first in line, the first to fall. Thanks to the few, the many were saved, and thanks to the fallen, we were able to stand erect once again.

"Of him and of his men, we might say, in David's words: 'They were swifter than eagles and more valiant than lions. . . .' Yonatan is slain on the high places. . . . I grieve for you Yonatan my brother, you were very dear to me. Your love was wonderful. . . ."

The distance in space between Entebbe and Jerusalem suddenly shortened the distance in time between Yonatan son of Saul and Yonatan son of Ben-Zion.

The same heroism in the man. The same grief in the heart of the people.

About the Author

Shimon Peres has held many leading Israeli government offices, including Minister of Posts and Transport, 1970–1974, and Minister of Defense, 1974–1977. Since the 1977 elections, he has been leader of the opposition Labor Party. He is also the author of *David's Sling.*